MYSTERIOUS ✦ DEATHS

Butch Cassidy

by Patricia Netzley

Lucent Books
P.O. Box 289011, San Diego, CA 92198-9011

These titles are included in the *Mysterious Deaths* series:

Butch Cassidy   The Little Princes in the Tower
Amelia Earhart   Malcolm X
John F. Kennedy   Marilyn Monroe
Abraham Lincoln   Mozart

*To my husband, children, and
parents, for believing.*

Cover design by Carl Franzen

Library of Congress Cataloging-in-Publication Data

Netzley, Patricia D.
    Butch Cassidy / by Patricia D. Netzley
        p. cm.—(Mysterious Deaths)
    Includes bibliographical references and index.
    Summary: A biography of the bandit who formed his own "Wild
Bunch" of outlaws which became famous for its robberies throughout
the Rocky Mountain states of the American West.
    ISBN 1-56006-266-5 (alk. paper)
    1. Cassidy, Butch, b. 1866—Juvenile literature.   2. Cassidy, Butch, b.
1866—Death and burial—Juvenile literature.   3. Outlaws—West (U.S.)
—Biography—Juvenile literature.   4. West (U.S.)—Biography—Juvenile
literature.   [1. Cassidy, Butch, b. 1866.   2. Robbers and outlaws.
3. West (U.S.)—Biography.]   I. Title.   II. Series.
F595.C362N48   1997
364.1'55'092—dc20   96-21507
[B]   CIP
                                                                   AC

Printed in the U.S.A.
Copyright © 1997 by Lucent Books, Inc.
P.O. Box 289011, San Diego, CA 92198-9011

Contents

Foreword
Haunting Human History   4

Introduction
Who Was Robert LeRoy Parker?   6

Chapter 1
A Dramatic Gunfight   27

Chapter 2
The Mystery Begins   37

Chapter 3
Exploring Other Identities   49

Chapter 4
Who Was William T. Phillips?   61

Chapter 5
Is the Mystery Solved?   76

For Further Reading   87

Works Consulted   89

Index   91

Picture Credits   95

About the Author   96

Haunting Human History

The *Mysterious Deaths* series focuses on nine individuals whose deaths have never been fully explained. Some are figures from the distant past; others are far more contemporary. Yet all of them remain fascinating as much for who they were and how they lived as for how they died. Their lives were characterized by fame and fortune, tragedy and triumph, secrets that led to acute vulnerability. Our enduring fascination with these stories, then, is due in part to the lives of the victims and in part to the array of conflicting facts and opinions, as well as the suspense, that surrounds their deaths.

Some of the people profiled in the *Mysterious Deaths* series were controversial political figures who lived and died in the public eye. John F. Kennedy, Abraham Lincoln, and Malcolm X were all killed in front of crowds as guards paid to protect them were unable to stop their murders. Despite all precautions, their assassins found ample opportunity to carry out their crimes. In each case, the assassins were tried and convicted. So what remains mysterious? As the reader will discover, everything.

The two women in the series, Marilyn Monroe and Amelia Earhart, are equally well remembered. Both died at the heights of their careers; both, from all appearances, had everything to live for. Yet their deaths have also been shrouded in mystery. While there are simple explanations—Monroe committed suicide, Earhart's plane crashed—the public has never been able to accept them. The more researchers dig into the deaths, the more mysterious evidence they unearth. Monroe's predilection for affairs with prominent politicians may have led to her death. Earhart, brash and cavalier, may have been involved in a government plot that collapsed around her. And these theories do not exhaust the mysterious possibilities that continue to puzzle researchers.

The circumstances of the deaths of the remaining figures in the *Mysterious Deaths* series—Richard III's nephews Edward and

Richard; the brilliant composer Wolfgang Mozart; and the infamous bank robber Butch Cassidy—are less well known but no less fascinating.

For example, what are almost surely the skeletons of the little princes Edward and Richard were found buried at the foot of a stairway in the Tower of London in 1674. To many, the discovery proved beyond a doubt that their evil uncle, Richard III, murdered them to attain the throne. Yet others find Richard wrongly accused, the obvious scapegoat. The mysterious tale of their deaths—full of dungeons, plots, and treachery—is still intriguing today.

In the history books, Wolfgang Mozart died in poverty from a consumptive-like disease. Yet there are reports and rumors, snatches of information culled from distant records, that Mozart may have died from a slow poisoning. Who could have wanted to murder the famous composer? And why?

Finally, bank robber Butch Cassidy's death couldn't have been less mysterious—shot to death by military police in Bolivia along with his companion, the Sundance Kid. Then why did members of Butch Cassidy's family and numerous others swear to have seen him, in full health, in the United States years after his supposed death?

These true-life whodunits are filled with tantalizing "what ifs?" What if Kennedy had used the bulletproof plastic hood that his Secret Servicemen had ready? What if Lincoln had decided not to attend the theater—which he did only to please his wife? What if Monroe's friend, Peter Lawford, receiving no answer to his persistent calls, had gone to her house, as he wanted to do? These questions frustrate us as well as testify to a haunting aspect of human history—the way that seemingly insignificant decisions can alter its course.

Who Was Robert LeRoy Parker?

George "Butch" Cassidy was a legendary bandit. From 1889 to 1908 he successfully stole over $500,000 from banks, trains, and company payrolls. In 1896 he formed his own band of outlaws, the Wild Bunch, which quickly became famous for its robberies throughout the Rocky Mountain states of the American West.

Butch was also noted for his skill with a gun. But though he was an expert marksman, he claimed that he never killed anyone. However, since people died while he was committing crimes, this seems unlikely. Yet, Butch's reputation for mercy, led many people to cheer whenever he escaped the law. Meanwhile, angry railroad owners used their power and money to push for his arrest.

Many lawmen tried to catch him. They tracked him across the country without success. Butch was a master of escape who outran or outsmarted all his pursuers. Newspapers reported his adventures with admiration.

Butch Was Admired

In fact, legend has it that everyone who knew Butch admired him. According to historian Charles Kelly, who wrote the first biography of Butch Cassidy in 1938, the outlaw was respected by friends and enemies alike.

Kelly interviewed many of Butch's contemporaries for his book, *The Outlaw Trail: A History of Butch Cassidy and His Wild Bunch*. In it he writes, "All old-timers . . . including officers who hunted him, were unanimous in saying, 'Butch Cassidy was one of the finest men I knew.'"

Kelly says that the outlaw was popular because of his disposition. Butch was even-tempered. He was never deliberately cruel. He was kind to children and always kept his word. Kelly writes: "[Butch Cassidy] has been called Utah's Robin Hood, not so much because of his generosity as because he was considered a 'gentleman outlaw.' He never drank to excess, was always courteous to women, was free with money when he had it, and extremely loyal to his friends."

A Religious Upbringing

Butch learned these traits from his parents, Maximillian and Ann Parker, who were members of the Mormon religion. Butch's grandparents had come to Utah from England in 1856 as part of a Mormon missionary movement.

Butch was the Parkers' eldest child. He was born on Friday, April 13, 1866, and named Robert LeRoy Parker. His parents called him LeRoy or Roy. All thirteen of his brothers and sisters called him Bob.

At the time LeRoy was born, Maximillian worked as a mail carrier. He took mail by horseback from Beaver, Utah, through the Circle Valley to Sanford Bench, Utah. The Circle Valley so impressed Maximillian that in 1879 he bought a 160-acre ranch there. It was just three miles south of the town of Circleville.

The ranch had a two-room log cabin where the entire family lived. LeRoy's sister, Lula Parker Betenson, describes her childhood home in her book, *Butch Cassidy, My Brother:*

> The log house already on the Parker Ranch in Circle Valley had a large room with a fireplace. This room served as a combination kitchen and living room, and a small room

An early photo of a frontier settlement in Utah. Butch Cassidy was born and raised in these surroundings.

was the bedroom. According to the prevailing custom, Mother covered the ceiling with large pieces of "factory," a cheap white cloth which gave the room a more liveable appearance and blocked out the crude roof beams. The rough floor was covered with homemade rag carpets stretched over straw for padding. Every year fresh straw was laid, and the carpets were cleaned outside, then tacked back in place. We filled bed ticks [mattress covers] with cornhusks or straw. Lace curtains, stiffly starched, hung at the windows. As soon as possible, Dad built on a large room to the east which became the kitchen and two rooms on the south as much-needed bedrooms. The granary, sheds, and corrals were all to the north of the house.

A Common Thief

The Parker ranch was not only humble, it was difficult to farm. Strong winds often blew away planted seeds and growing sprouts. A harsh winter killed all but two of the family's cattle.

Still, LeRoy and his siblings enjoyed their childhood. They caught grasshoppers, tied string to the insects' legs, and raced them. They built rafts and floated them on a nearby pond. They held mock rodeos, roping and riding calves and horses. They also kept a variety of pets, including magpies. LeRoy trained his bird to talk and made a cage for it out of willow strips.

But, the Parker ranch continued to fail. Finally Maximillian decided to farm a neighboring piece of unclaimed property. In those days, anyone could become the owner of unclaimed land adjacent to his house by farming it himself. This was called homesteading.

The Parkers expected a rich harvest from the homesteaded land. Their seeds were growing well, and it looked as though their hard times would end. Then another man claimed the land was his. Maximillian knew this was impossible. He went to the bishop of the Mormon Church, who settled all disputes in the area, expecting his homesteading claim to be upheld. Instead the bishop ruled against the Parkers.

Maximillian was furious. He felt the bishop had decided against him only because he sometimes did not go to church. He told his children that the Mormon Church had stolen his property like a common thief.

Honest Butch

John F. Kelly was a cowboy who knew Butch Cassidy. He verifies the outlaw's honesty in James Horan's book, Desperate Men.

"I returned to Forsythe to work for a cow outfit. Shortly after Butch rode up. He asked for a loan of $25 to help him get to Butte, Montana. In the fall of 1887, I received a letter from him. When I opened it one hundred dollars in cash fell out. The letter said simply, 'If you don't know how I got this, you will soon learn someday.' "

Young LeRoy shared his father's anger. The boy stopped going to church services and religious classes. He spoke harsh words about the powerful Mormons.

Many historians believe that this incident was the source of Butch Cassidy's lack of respect for the law. They say he grew to equate banks and railroads with the Mormon Church. In her book, Butch's sister supports this theory:

> The more [LeRoy] saw, the more disgusted he became with the laws that were supposed to protect people and their rights. He came to feel they protected only the man who already had more money than he knew what to do with and more herds than he could keep track of. He couldn't forget how his own parents' land had been jumped. The underdog always got the raw end of a deal. The little homesteader, more often than not, was driven off by the big man who had enough cash to see that the land office was on his side and that he ended up with huge tracts of choice rangeland.

> From his own observations, [LeRoy] felt that banks and railroad companies were also out to take away the land from the poor man to use for their own greedy purposes. His bitterness against money factions deepened.

Turning to Crime

LeRoy had reason to be angry. His life changed after his family lost their homesteaded land. His father took a job hauling wood in the

Butch Cassidy as a young man. Early on, Cassidy grew frustrated and angry at what he perceived to be the unfair laws and tenets of society. Did his disillusionment with the Mormon Church contribute to his outlaw behavior?

nearby town of Frisco. His mother went to work twelve miles away, in the dairy of a ranch owned by Jim Marshall. LeRoy went to work there too, as a ranch hand.

He quickly became friends with a cowboy named Mike Cassidy. Cassidy taught LeRoy everything he knew—riding, roping, shooting, and stealing. Mike was an accomplished thief who had stolen both horses and cattle. But according to historian Charles Kelly, such activities were not unusual. In his book, *The Outlaw Trail*, he writes:

> If one believes old-timers' stories, about half the inhabitants of Circle Valley at that time were connected in some way with cattle rustling. To obtain a start in the cattle business, young men went out on the desert or into the hills and put their brand on any unmarked animals they found. It was an easy matter to separate a calf from its mother, when it became technically a maverick [unbranded range animal]. Branding calves was a sort of game played by all cattlemen, the winner being the one who got his mark on the largest number.

Mike Cassidy had several partners. They were local ranchers who kept Mike's stolen, rebranded cattle in their corrals until he could move them to a nearby secluded canyon. When Mike had gathered enough animals there, he took them to Colorado to sell. LeRoy Parker helped Mike Cassidy herd his livestock on at least one occasion.

Everything went well until several men recognized their cattle in the ranchers' corrals. They saw that the animals had been re-branded. They demanded an explanation and called in the town constable.

Mike's partners denied stealing the cattle. They said they had bought the livestock from someone else. If anyone had stolen the cattle, it was the person who had sold them. They produced a bill of sale to prove their innocence. It bore the signature of Robert LeRoy Parker.

The constable drew up a warrant for Parker's arrest. But before anyone could catch him, LeRoy rode out of town. He changed his name to George Cassidy, in honor of his old friend Mike Cassidy, and went to Telluride, Colorado.

A New Nickname

In Telluride, George Cassidy worked for a while as a mule-train operator for a mining company. Then he returned to ranching. He became a cowboy drifter, moving from ranch to ranch throughout Colorado and Wyoming. He never stayed any place very long.

Somewhere during his travels he started using the name Butch instead of George. Historians disagree about the source of this nickname. Some say Cassidy got it while working as a butcher. Others say it came from an episode with a tricky pistol. According to E. Richard Churchill in his book, *The McCartys: They Rode with Butch Cassidy*,

> It was during the extended flight which followed [Butch's first bank robbery] that Butch Cassidy got his famous nickname according to [partner-in-crime Matt] Warner. It seems the group had a needle gun with a terrific recoil. The weapon was nicknamed "butch."
>
> Cassidy was standing on a rock at the edge of a shallow lake in eastern Utah with the weapon in question. Sensing a golden opportunity Matt challenged Cassidy to hit a rock in the lake. Cassidy accepted the dare, was knocked backwards into the muddy water by the recoil, and carried the name Butch ever after.

Other writers attribute the name Butch to the time Cassidy worked as a butcher in Wyoming. This is just another of the many instances when "you pays your money and you takes your choice."

The First Bank Robbery

Butch's first bank robbery occurred on June 24, 1889. By this time he had joined up with Matt Warner and Tom McCarty, two notorious outlaws who were planning to rob the San Miguel Valley bank in Telluride, Colorado. The bank handled large payrolls from local mining companies.

From his days of working in Telluride, Butch knew the town and its bank well. He helped his partners plan the robbery and devise an escape route. The outlaws hid fresh horses at measured intervals along the route. Their plan was to change to new mounts just as their old ones were growing tired.

Before the robbery they added a fourth man to their group, Bill Maddern. Maddern's job was to act as lookout. He would wait outside the bank, hold the first group of horses, and watch for lawmen.

The gang's plan seemed foolproof. Still, Butch wanted to practice the first part of his getaway. About a month before the holdup, he went to Telluride with his favorite horse and worked on his escape. E. Richard Churchill explains:

> [Several] residents [around Telluride] later recalled seeing Cassidy practice with one of [Tom] McCarty's race horses. He trained the horse to stand perfectly still while he raced toward it and jumped into the saddle. Instantly the horse broke into a gallop which Cassidy held it to for a mile. The horse was then halted and the entire procedure repeated. Miners laughed at the crazy cowboy and paid no future attention until their bank's resources were suddenly depleted. Then they recalled Cassidy's training program and allowed as it wasn't so crazy after all.

When the day of the robbery finally came, Butch's planning and practicing paid off. The gang of outlaws was successful. According to a June 27, 1889, issue of a Denver newspaper, the *Rocky Mountain News*,

The main street of Telluride, Colorado, around the time Cassidy fled there to avoid being caught for cattle rustling. The steepled building (left of center) is the San Miguel Valley Bank—the site of Cassidy's first bank robbery.

The robbery of the San Miguel Valley bank of Telluride on Monday by four daring cowboys . . . is one of the boldest affairs of the kind ever known in southern Colorado. The robbers secured about $20,000. . . . They came to Telluride two or three days prior to the robbery, put their horses in Searle's stable and proceeded to take in the town, drinking and spending money freely. In this way they secured the information they desired and acted accordingly. The bank employs one clerk as assistant to the cashier. During the morning the robbers took their horses from the stable, paid their bill and then visited two or three saloons, watching the bank in the meantime. Soon cashier Painter stepped out to do some collecting and the four rode over to the bank, and leaving their horses in charge of one of the number, two remained on the sidewalk and the fourth entered the bank and presented a check to the clerk.

As the latter was bending over the desk examining the check this party grabbed him around the neck, pulling his face down on the desk, at the same time admonishing the surprised official to keep quiet on pain of instant death. He then called to his partners on the sidewalk, saying, "Come

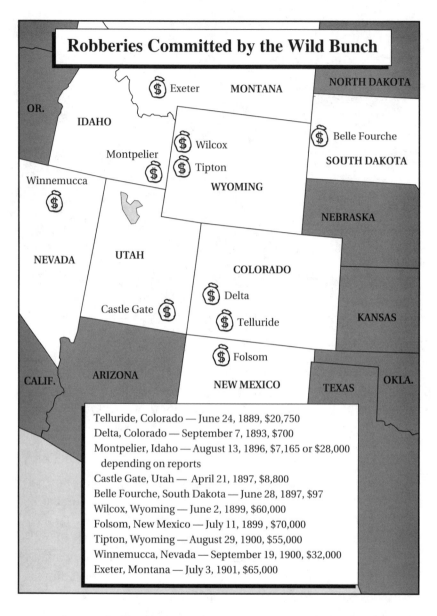

Robberies Committed by the Wild Bunch

Telluride, Colorado — June 24, 1889, $20,750
Delta, Colorado — September 7, 1893, $700
Montpelier, Idaho — August 13, 1896, $7,165 or $28,000
   depending on reports
Castle Gate, Utah — April 21, 1897, $8,800
Belle Fourche, South Dakota — June 28, 1897, $97
Wilcox, Wyoming — June 2, 1899, $60,000
Folsom, New Mexico — July 11, 1899 , $70,000
Tipton, Wyoming — August 29, 1900, $55,000
Winnemucca, Nevada — September 19, 1900, $32,000
Exeter, Montana — July 3, 1901, $65,000

on, boys, it's all right." The boys came in and cleaned up all available cash amounting to $20,750, while their comrade held the trembling clerk over the desk by the neck. When their work was complete the clerk was released and fell in a heap on the floor. Surveying the quaking mass of humanity the robber said he had a notion to shoot him anyway for being such a coward, and then joining his comrades they mounted their horses and rode leisurely away.

When they had ridden a couple of blocks they spurred their horses into a gallop, gave a yell, discharged their revolvers and dashed away. It was fifteen minutes after this demonstration, of which little notice was taken, that Mr. Painter, on returning to his bank, found his clerk Shee too agitated to give a correct account of the affair.

[Shee's] greeting to the cashier was, "It's all gone, all gone," and such proved to be the case.

Ride for the Hideouts

After the robbery, a posse led by Sheriff J. A. Beattie chased the bandits. Just when the sheriff thought he would catch up with Butch's gang, they changed to fresh horses and outdistanced him. On one occasion they pulled ahead through another clever tactic. They sent a riderless horse to disrupt the posse. In his book, *The McCartys: They Rode with Butch Cassidy*, E. Richard Churchill explains:

[Matt] Warner said [that after robbing the bank at Telluride] the trio covered thirty-five miles in two and a half hours of wild riding toward the Mancos Mountains. The one thing certain about the ride is that when pursuit got too close at one point Matt roped an Indian pony which was so unfortunate as to be near at the moment. The wily outlaw tied a bush to the horse's tail and set the pony loose at a gallop toward the oncoming posse. The noise of the pony crashing through the timber and the dust raised by the brush completely demoralized the posse and gave the three time to make good their escape.

Matt, Tom, and Butch soon outdistanced the posse. They then headed for their hideout at Brown's Park. Originally called Brown's Hole, the place had long been a favorite of outlaws running from the law. It was a desolate canyon area about forty miles square, half in Utah and half in Colorado, divided by the Green River and surrounded by mountains. On one of these mountains is a spot still known as Cassidy Point.

As the name suggests, Butch spent a lot of time at Cassidy Point. Robert Redford explains why in his book, *The Outlaw Trail: A Journey Through Time:*

[In Butch's time] there was a cabin up on the Point, cleverly constructed beneath an overhanging ledge of rock and well out of sight, but commanding a view of the park for miles in all directions. A trail led up to the Point from the Crouse Ranch below. Mrs. Crouse often cooked meals for the men hiding out up there, and her daughter Minnie . . . carried the food up to the men. Minnie . . . was a girlfriend of Butch Cassidy.

When Butch's gang eventually left Brown's Park, they went to another favorite outlaw hideout, Robbers Roost in Utah. Robbers Roost was in an area of canyons and plateaus, where caves could substitute for living quarters. In *The Outlaw Trail*, Robert Redford describes this area well:

Outlaws would rustle their cattle into the Roost, which was a five-mile circular flat that had lookout points on all sides. The Roost is identifiable by two flat-topped buttes on the edge of the flat, facing east and north. It provided the outlaws with caves in which to store their weapons, bunkhouses, saloons and such "essentials" as disguised hollowed-out trees for the posting of letters and messages. Isolated from settlements by miles of desert and box canyons, it was almost inaccessible except to the few who

Lawmen Helped Out

Sometimes Cassidy paid local lawmen to look the other way while they robbed a bank. In Larry Pointer's book, In Search of Butch Cassidy, *Jim Clark, town constable of Telluride, Colorado, tells of his involvement in the outlaw's first major bank robbery.*

"The fellers who held up the bank were friends of mine. They told me their plans and said that if I made a point of being out of town at the time of the robbery they would give me a fair share of the take. They agreed to hide it under a big log along the trail on which they planned to make their getaway. They were true to their word and left me this roll of bills amounting to about $2,200."

Robbers Roost in Utah reveals the canyons, plateaus, and cavelike areas that became favorite hiding places for Cassidy and his gang.

knew the route, and many lawmen brave or foolish enough to penetrate the refuge were lost in the mazes or perished from thirst. Because the outlaws knew where the vital springs were, they could survive.

Butch and his partners stayed at Robbers Roost for several days before splitting up. Then Butch returned to his former life as a cowboy. Once again he moved from ranch to ranch, never staying any place very long. Finally he ended up in Rock Springs, Wyoming, where he took a job as a butcher.

For a while it looked as though Butch would stay out of trouble with the law. Then one day he was accused of stealing money from a drunk in a saloon. He was arrested and thrown in jail. At his trial he was found innocent, but the experience affected him deeply. It turned him into a very angry man. In his book, *The Outlaw Trail*, Charles Kelly says:

There is little doubt of his innocence, for during his whole career he never stooped to petty thievery. When the case came to trial no evidence could be produced against him and he was acquitted. But the circumstances surrounding the case, his confinement in jail, and the injustice of his arrest for the lowest of crimes made him so bitter that when he left the courtroom he cursed the officers, the judge, the town of Rock Springs, the county of Sweetwater, and the entire state of Wyoming. He swore they would sooner or later feel the sharp edge of his vengeance. Men in the courtroom paid little heed to the angry cowboy at that time but were often reminded of his threat in after years. Cassidy never forgot that day.

Return to Crime

Because of this incident, Butch left Rock Springs and became a cowboy again. He also returned to a life of crime. While working at various ranches in Wyoming, he stole cattle from everyone but his current employer.

The ranch owners soon realized what was happening. In *The Outlaw Trail*, Charles Kelly says: "In a very short time [Butch] was known as the leader of the rustlers and for that very reason big ranchers were anxious to have him on their payrolls. They knew that as long as he took their money their herds would not be molested. It was cheap insurance against cattle stealing."

Butch's activities expanded to include horse stealing. He was a successful thief until someone noticed he had stolen horses in his corral. On April 11, 1892, Deputy Bob Calverly went to arrest the outlaw.

Butch did not go quietly. According to Calverly, Cassidy reached for his gun when he saw the lawman. On June 16, 1939, the *Wyoming State Tribune* printed a letter by Calverly that stated:

I told [Cassidy] that I had a warrant for him and he said: "Well, get to shooting," and with that we both pulled our guns. I put the barrel of my revolver almost to his stomach, but it missed three times but owing to the fact that there was another man between us, he failed to hit me. The fourth time I snapped the gun it went off and the bullet hit him in the upper part of the forehead and felled him. I then had him and he made no further resistance.

The Wyoming State Penitentiary

Cassidy was jailed and ordered to stand trial as a horse thief. He insisted that this time he was innocent. He had actually bought the stolen horses from another man. Nonetheless, on July 15, 1894, he was found guilty and sentenced to two years in the Wyoming State Penitentiary. It was the only time he would ever be convicted of a crime.

After serving a year and a half of his sentence, Butch Cassidy was released from prison. Some historians say that the governor of Wyoming pardoned him in exchange for his promise that he would never rob a Wyoming bank. Others believe he was released early as a reward for good behavior. All records indicate he was a model prisoner.

The Wild Bunch

It was immediately after his release from prison that Cassidy formed the Wild Bunch. The Wild Bunch was the largest band of outlaws in the Old West, sometimes numbering over two hundred men. Many of its members had once belonged to other gangs.

The Wild Bunch operated out of Brown's Park and Robbers Roost, as well as a famous hideout in Wyoming called Hole-in-the-Wall. Hole-in-the-Wall had been used by outlaws for years because of its unique geography. It was a valley bordered on the east by a

Cassidy's release order from the Wyoming State Penitentiary explains that he was pardoned.

19

Members of the Wild Bunch: (from left to right) Harry Longabaugh (Sundance Kid), Will Carver, Ben Kilpatrick, Harvey Logan (Kid Curry), Robert Parker (Butch Cassidy). The group was also called the Hole-in-the-Wall gang because they met at an opening in a line of cliffs.

line of cliffs called the Great Red Wall, which had only one small opening. In his book Robert Redford explains the significance of this opening and what lay behind it:

> Its penetration in the wall is so small that two men with Winchester rifles could hold off an entire army. Beyond the opening . . . there was no access to Hole-in-the-Wall from the east. To the west, south, and part of the north extended a sea of grassy plains that provided ample grazing for the outlaws' stolen herds. Here the cattle would idle and be fattened on abundant hay and then rebranded for illicit sale elsewhere.

Robberies and Dynamite

The Wild Bunch was an ever changing group. However, certain men were always members: Elzy Lay, who was Butch's closest friend, Bill Carver, Harvey Logan, Kid Curry, Ben Kilpatrick, and Harry Longabaugh, also known as the Sundance Kid.

Some historians think Harvey Logan and Kid Curry were the same man. However, Edna Robison of Hanksville, Utah, who knew

Penitentiary Records

The Wyoming State Penitentiary maintains records of past prisoners. The listing for criminals received on July 15, 1894, includes the following information about Butch Cassidy. It is interesting to note that he lied about his place of birth, probably to protect his family.

"Wyoming State Prison number 187; Name, George 'Butch' Cassidy; Received 7-15-94; Age, 27; Nativity, New York City; Occupation, cowboy; Height, 5'9"; Complexion, light; Hair, dark flaxen; Eyes, blue; Wife, no; Parents, not known; Children, no; Religion, none; Habits of life, intemperate; Education, common school; Relations address, not known; Weight, 165 pounds; Marks scars: features, regular, small deep set eyes, 2 cut scars on back of head, small red scar under left eye, red mark on left side of back, small brown mole on calf of left leg, good build."

Butch Cassidy's prison record gives his physical description.

the Wild Bunch, said they were not. Lula Parker Betenson, in her book, *Butch Cassidy, My Brother*, quotes Robison as saying: "I can testify that Kid Curry and Harvey Logan were two separate men, because they used to stay here with us and feed their horses, and we knew them very well."

Many other things about the Wild Bunch are uncertain. For example, no one knows for sure how many crimes they committed. However, most historians think their first robbery occurred on August 13, 1896. At that time, Butch, Elzy Lay, and Bub Meeks stole either $7,165, according to the bank teller, or $28,000 (according to the outlaws) from the bank at Montpelier, Idaho.

Most historians believe that the Wild Bunch's first train robbery occurred near Wilcox, Wyoming, on June 2, 1899. Witnesses to that robbery say that Butch and several other men stopped the Overland Flyer of the Union Pacific Railroad by blocking its tracks. They then sought its express car, which contained metal safes filled with money.

The outlaws found the car locked. Messenger Earnest C. Woodcock had barred the door from inside, so Butch decided to dynamite it. Unfortunately he used too much gunpowder. The blast knocked Woodcock unconscious. (He later recovered and, in fact, encountered Butch Cassidy again during a train robbery at Tipton, Wyoming.)

Without Woodcock, there was no way to learn the combination that opened the safes. Butch quickly decided to dynamite them too. This time the blast destroyed the entire railroad car, and money scattered everywhere.

A train car shows the effects of a recent robbery.

The Pinkertons

Now that the Wild Bunch had begun robbing trains, their life became more difficult. The wealthy railroad owners did not like having their business threatened. The express companies that sent money by rail were equally unhappy. These two groups tried everything to stop the outlaws. They reinforced their railroad cars and their safes against dynamite. They added extra guards to their trains. They also sent out certain trains as traps, with lawmen instead of passengers inside their cars.

Edward H. Harriman

When E. H. Harriman took over the Union Pacific Railroad in 1898, he improved the traps. He created special railroad cars that could hold armed men on horseback, and stationed them so that they could be pulled to the scene of a train robbery in less than an hour. The horsemen would then leap out to pursue outlaws before they had gotten very far.

Harriman also hired a special group of men to end all train robberies. He paid agents from the Pinkerton National Detective Agency to catch Butch Cassidy and his Wild Bunch.

The Pinkerton National Detective Agency specialized in train robberies, but it investigated all kinds of crimes. It was founded in 1850 by Allan Pinkerton, a Scottish barrel maker who turned to law enforcement after capturing a gang of counterfeiters in his hometown.

Pinkerton was a deputy sheriff in Chicago, Illinois, before establishing his detective agency there. In the beginning he ran the agency himself, but later his two sons, Robert and William, took over. The elder Pinkerton died in 1884 after writing a book called *Thirty Years a Detective*, which described his long career as a private investigator.

Under Allan Pinkerton's leadership, the Pinkerton National Detective Agency had many successes. In 1861 its agents foiled an attempt to assassinate President Abraham Lincoln in Baltimore, Maryland. In 1866, they caught the outlaws who stole $700,000 from the Adams Express Company. In 1876, the agency presented

Pinkerton Agent Charles Siringo

According to Charles Kelly in his book, The Outlaw Trail, *Pinkerton agent Charles Siringo once managed to infiltrate the Wild Bunch. Butch eventually discovered the detective's true identity, and Siringo fled—but not before uncovering valuable information.*

"[Charles Siringo] disguised himself as a cowpuncher, posed as an outlaw, and actually joined the Wild Bunch, learning their plans and obtaining a copy of their secret code. Through the use of that code he broke up plans of their first train robbery and gave the syndicate a year's setback. Thereafter they used messengers only and never put anything in writing."

evidence that the Molly Maguires, a secret organization of coal miners, had been conducting terrorist activities against mine owners. A Pinkerton detective, James McParlan, lived undercover among the Maguires for three years to gather information against them.

Pinkerton detectives were carefully trained to do this kind of work. Many were able to infiltrate outlaw gangs and learn about upcoming robberies. Others were more talented in pursuit. They would follow an outlaw until they caught him, killed him, or had proof that he was already dead.

Neither Butch Cassidy nor his men wanted to be the target of a Pinkerton pursuit. In his book, *Last of the Bandit Riders*, Hole-in-the-Wall outlaw Matt Warner tells how horrible it was to be followed by the detectives:

> It was hell proper. It wasn't a case of just one outfit of deputies trailing us, but posses was out scouring the whole country, and we was running into fresh outfits every little while and had to suddenly change our direction, or dodge into a rock or timber hideout, or backtrack, or follow long strips of bare sandstone where we wouldn't leave tracks, or wade up or down streams long distances so they would lose our tracks. We had to put into practice all the tricks we had learned as cowboys and learn all the new tricks outlaws had to know to stay alive.

With the Pinkertons after him, Butch Cassidy realized his luck was running out. Sooner or later he would be caught and imprisoned. His worries increased after his friend Elzy Lay was wounded and captured during a train robbery in July 1899. Butch told many people that he wanted to stop being an outlaw so the same thing would not happen to him.

South America

Because of Butch's fears, the Wild Bunch committed its last crime on July 3, 1901. Butch Cassidy, the Sundance Kid, and a few others robbed a train near Exeter, Montana, of approximately $65,000. Then Butch and Sundance said goodbye to their associates. They were heading for South America, where surely no Pinkerton detective would follow them.

William A. Pinkerton (center) with two special agents in the typical garb used for scouting outlaws. The Pinkerton agency was known for its relentless pursuit of criminals.

The posse from the Pinkerton agency that pursued the Wild Bunch. The persistence of the posse made Cassidy, Sundance, and Etta Place flee for South America.

The two first traveled to New York with Sundance's girlfriend Etta Place. After three weeks of sightseeing there, Sundance and Etta boarded a luxury ocean liner for Buenos Aires, Argentina. Meanwhile, Butch took a cattle boat to Liverpool, England, sailing from there to Argentina on a passenger ship.

In South America the three reunited. They bought a ranch in Argentina and for a while they worked it honestly. Then they returned to crime, robbing several South American banks and at least one train.

Eventually Butch and Sundance got jobs as payroll guards for the Concordia Tin Mines in Bolivia. Butch's last known letter, dated February 16, 1908, was addressed to the manager of the Concordia Tin Mines. It was a brief note about scheduling and ended with the words "every thing is OK here as far as I know."

After that, what happened to Butch Cassidy is a mystery.

1 A Dramatic Gunfight

On April 23, 1930, the *Washington Post* newspaper displayed the headline BUTCH IS DEAD. The accompanying article reported a story that had just been published in *Elks Magazine*.

The story's author was poet Arthur Chapman. He claimed he had discovered the fate of legendary train robbers Butch Cassidy and Harry Longabaugh, also known as the Sundance Kid. In dramatic style, Chapman described the outlaws' adventures in the United States and their escape to South America. He said that their last holdup occurred when they stole the payroll of the Aramayo mines near Quechisla, Bolivia, in 1909.

Then Chapman revealed what happened to the outlaws. According to Charles Kelly in his book, *The Outlaw Trail*, Chapman wrote:

A few weeks after this holdup two heavily armed Americans, on jaded [exhausted] mules, rode into the patio of the police station at the Indian village of San Vicente, Bolivia, and demanded something to eat.

It was not an unusual demand, for the police station was also an inn, and there was no place else in the village where wayfarers could find food and shelter.

After making it known that they intended to pass the night at the station, the strangers stripped their saddles, blankets and rifles from their mules. They piled their equipment in a room at one side of the little courtyard which was soon to become a shambles. Then they sat at a table in a room across the patio and called for a speedy serving of food and liquor.

One of the men was Butch Cassidy and the other was Harry Longabaugh. After the Aramayo mines remittance [payroll]

Butch Cassidy

holdup, the bandits had proceeded to Tupiza, where they took employment with a transportation outfit. Learning that they had been identified as the perpetrators of the Aramayo holdup, they hurriedly departed for Uyuni, Bolivia.

The constable in charge of the station at San Vicente happened to catch sight of one of the strangers' mules, then rolling in the dust of the courtyard to relieve his saddle-galled [worn] back. He recognized the animal as having belonged to a friend of his—a muleteer [mule driver] who was helping transport the Aramayo mines' remittance when the holdup took place.

How did these Americans across the courtyard come into possession of that mule? They were rough-looking fellows, with stubby beards and battered clothes. Maybe they had something to do with the holdup. If they were bandits, they were careless, as their rifles were leaning against the adobe wall in the room which held their saddles. It would be easy to capture these hungry gentry [gentlemen] and inquire into matters. There was a company of Bolivian cavalry just outside of town. The constable would send an Indian messenger to the captain. Then the Americans would have to explain how they came into possession of that mule.

On receipt of the message the Bolivian captain brought up his command and quietly surrounded the station. Then the captain himself walked into the room where Cassidy and Longabaugh were eating and drinking.

"Surrender, señors," came the demand from the brave captain.

The outlaws leaped to their feet. Longabaugh was drunk, but Cassidy, always a canny [restrained] drinker, was in complete command of his senses.

The captain had drawn his revolver when he entered the room. Before he could fire, Cassidy shot from the hip. The captain fell dead and Cassidy and Longabaugh stationed themselves where they could command a view of the patio.

A sergeant and a picked body of cavalrymen rushed through the gate, calling upon the outlaws to surrender. Revolvers blazed from door and window and men began to stagger and fall in the courtyard. The first to die was the sergeant who had sought to rescue his captain.

Cassidy and Longabaugh were firing rapidly and with deadly effect. Those of the detachment who remained on their feet were firing in return. Bullets sank into the thick adobe walls or whistled through the window and door. Other soldiers began firing from behind the shelter of the courtyard wall.

"Keep me covered, Butch," called Longabaugh. "I'll get our rifles."

Shooting as he went, Longabaugh lurched into the courtyard. If he could only reach the rifles and ammunition which they had so thoughtlessly laid aside, the fight would be something the outlaws would welcome.

Blood was settling in little pools about the courtyard. The sergeant and most of his file of soldiers were stretched out dead. A few wounded were trying to crawl to safety. The mules had broken their halters and galloped out of the yard, among them the animal which had been the indirect cause of the battle.

Soldiers were firing through the open gate and from all other vantage points outside the wall. Longabaugh got halfway across the courtyard and fell, desperately wounded, but not before he had effectively emptied his six-shooter.

When Cassidy saw his partner fall, he rushed into the courtyard. Bullets rained about him as he ran to Longabaugh's side. Some of the shots found their mark, but Cassidy, though wounded, managed to pick up Longabaugh and stagger back to the house with his heavy burden.

Cassidy saw that Longabaugh was mortally wounded. Furthermore, it was going to be impossible to carry on the battle much longer unless the rifles and ammunition could be reached. Cassidy made several attempts to cross the courtyard. At each attempt he was wounded and driven back.

The battle now settled into a siege. Night came on, and men fired at the red flashes from weapons. There were spaces of increasing length between Cassidy's shots. He had only a few cartridges left. Longabaugh's cartridge belt was empty. So was the dead Bolivian captain's.

The soldiers, about 9:00 or 10:00 o'clock in the evening, heard two shots fired in the bullet-riddled station. Then no more shots came. Perhaps it was a ruse to lure them into the patio within range of those deadly revolvers. The soldiers kept on firing all through the night and during the next morning.

About noon an officer and a detachment of soldiers rushed through the patio and into the station. They found Longabaugh and Cassidy dead. Cassidy had fired a bullet into Longabaugh's head, and had used his last cartridge to kill himself.

In the pack saddles of the bandits was found intact the money that had been taken in the Aramayo mines remittance holdup, besides a large sum in pounds sterling, gold, which had been taken in the holdup of the Bolivian railway. Also in the equipment of the bandits was found a considerable quantity of antiseptic drugs, field glasses, and a beautiful Tiffany watch which Cassidy was known to have bought in New York when enroute for Buenos Aires.

Chapman's Story Accepted as Fact

Arthur Chapman's article was the first published account of Butch Cassidy's death. People who read the story declared the Bolivian gunfight a fitting end for such a notorious outlaw. How glorious it was that he had died in such a spectacular shoot-out! How amazing that Butch and Sundance had decided to end their own lives rather than face capture!

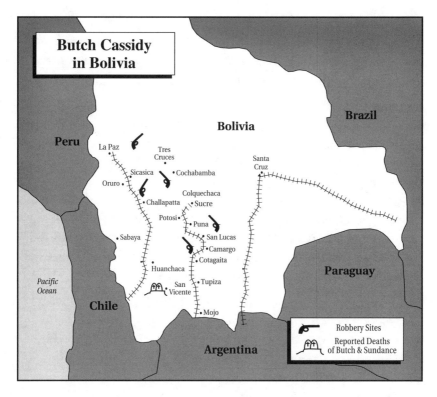

**Butch Cassidy
in Bolivia**

Bolivia

Brazil

Peru

La Paz

Tres
Cruces

Santa
Cruz

Sicasica

Cochabamba

Oruro

Colquechaca

Challapatta   Sucre

Potosi

Puna

Sabaya

San Lucas

Camargo

Cotagaita

Huanchaca

Paraguay

Pacific
Ocean

San
Vicente

Tupiza

Chile

Mojo

Robbery Sites

Reported Deaths
of Butch & Sundance

Argentina

Historian Charles Kelly especially marveled at the way the two men had fought during their final hours. In his 1938 book, *The Outlaw Trail,* he writes: "Cassidy and Longabaugh had made good soldiers out of twenty Bolivians, and had wounded twice that many. Two men with six-shooters against a company of soldiers with rifles! It was just the sort of finish one might have expected— the sort they would themselves have desired."

It was a perfect story—perhaps a little *too* perfect. But like Charles Kelly, most people accepted it as fact. The Pinkerton National Detective Agency even relied on Chapman's article to end their search for Butch Cassidy. They had heard rumors about the outlaw's death ever since 1909. Now they believed they had accurate information about what had happened to him. In 1930 they declared Butch Cassidy dead and closed their files on him.

Historian Larry Pointer feels that people believed the story because they wanted to. In his book, *In Search of Butch Cassidy,* he says:

[Chapman's] account of Butch Cassidy went unchallenged because people wanted to believe it. With sensational style, contrived dialogue, and lurid detail, he gave a Depression-weary public an escape to the fantasy land of the dime novels of their youth. He painted the west just the way Americans had grown to believe it really was. It was the stuff of which story books are made.

Pointer does not blame the general public for wanting to believe that the outlaw died in a glorious shootout. However, he criticizes historians who repeated the unconfirmed story. Pointer believes that historians have a special responsibility to search out the truth.

Pointer particularly faults historian Charles Kelly, whose book, *The Outlaw Trail*, was for many years "considered the final word on the life of Butch Cassidy." Pointer says that while Kelly was writing *The Outlaw Trail*, he ignored any evidence that suggested Chapman's story might be false. Pointer explains:

> In Wyoming, some five years after [Chapman's article was published], rumors began circulating that Butch Cassidy had not died in South America, but had returned to the United States and had even revisited old Wyoming friends from his outlaw days. . . .
>
> Kelly was convinced of the authenticity of the legendary battle at San Vicente. The Utah author had interviewed Wyoming pioneers and was aware of the claims Cassidy had returned to visit his old haunts, yet he dismissed the accounts as fiction.

Kelly's book does include a chapter entitled "Is Butch Cassidy Dead?" It discusses several rumors that Butch Cassidy lived past the year 1909. But Kelly concludes that these rumors are probably false. He says it is far more likely that Butch Cassidy died in South America.

Kelly bases this conclusion on Cassidy's love for his family. In *The Outlaw Trail* he states: "If George LeRoy Parker, the Mormon cowboy-outlaw, [was] still alive, it seems strange he never returned to Cir-

Lula Parker Betenson

Butch's Rigid Code

In her book, Butch Cassidy, My Brother, *Lula Parker Betenson describes her brother as a man of good character, despite his life of crime.*

"[Butch] had a rigid code, one he never violated even in the tightest spots. He was loyal to his friends, his family and his employers. I have often been informed by his associates that he was courteous and respectful to all women and that any girl was safe with him. He was kind to animals and was a fine horseman. He was a man's man. He commanded respect from them all, even those who were on the opposite side of the law. All his life children adored him. He had a natural way with them. Wherever [he] went, the farmers and ranchers welcomed him. He was pleasant and witty, good company, trustworthy, compassionate."

cleville, Utah, to visit his old father, . . . who died on July 28, 1938, at the age of ninety-four."

Butch's Sister Speaks Out

But Butch's sister, Lula Parker Betenson, says that he did visit his father. In her book, *Butch Cassidy, My Brother,* she says that Butch showed up at the family ranch in 1925. After that, he corresponded with his siblings. Betenson adds that there was a reason Butch did not see his father just before the old man's death. She explains: "Robert LeRoy Parker died in the Northwest in the fall of 1937, a year before Dad died."

In addition, Betenson insists that many stories about her brother are untrue. Like Larry Pointer, she faults Charles Kelly and other historians for repeating such misinformation. She says:

Books written about [Butch Cassidy] have been replete with [full of] errors borrowed back and forth from one author to another, mixed with the legends handed down by word of mouth, and embellished to spin a more sensational tale. But once the legend or half-truth appears in print, it is translated into absolute fact by the reader. The mistakes are compounded and are then generally considered irrefutable. One author makes a statement, true or false, without quoting his source; he, then, becomes the source for those who come after him. Few writers have documented specific details, and the reader is left to wonder where fact ends and fiction begins.

The stories became wilder and wilder. My brother was given credit for robberies which were committed at almost the same time, but many hundreds of miles apart, in the days of horseback travel. He would certainly have needed wings—and we know he was no angel.

A Popular Movie

Historian Kent Ladd Steckmesser agrees that there is much misinformation about Butch Cassidy's life. He says that stories about famous outlaws are often untrue. In his book, *Western Outlaws: The "Good Badman" in Fact, Film, and Folklore*, he states: "Much of the material about Cassidy is folkloric rather than historical. He was the subject of oral traditions comparable to those about [Western outlaw] Jesse James."

However, Steckmesser does not find much fault with Charles Kelly's book, *The Outlaw Trail*. He calls Kelly "a conscientious researcher." Instead, he blames a 1969 movie for most of the misinformation about Butch Cassidy. Steckmesser says this movie,

Newspapers Inaccurate

After the August 13, 1896, robbery of the bank in Montpelier, Idaho, Lula Parker Betenson read conflicting reports as to whether Cassidy and Elzy Lay were the ones who committed the crime. In Butch Cassidy, My Brother, *she writes:*

"Such was the maze of information and misinformation sifting through to us about [Butch Cassidy]. It was usually very confusing, and, of course, I have no way of straightening out his escapades which have been so widely published. Readers accept newspaper stories as factual in every detail, when many times they are not. Yet newspapers were our only source of information."

In a scene from Butch Cassidy and the Sundance Kid, *Robert Redford as Sundance (left), tries to help a wounded Cassidy crawl to safety. Is the movie's depiction of the pair's end accurate?*

entitled *Butch Cassidy and the Sundance Kid,* reached far more people than Kelly's book did. Written by William Goldman, the Twentieth Century Fox film starring Paul Newman and Robert Redford was so popular that within ten years it had grossed $75 million.

At the beginning of the movie is the statement, "Not that it matters, but most of what follows is true." Steckmesser disagrees with this statement. He says that the movie is filled with inaccuracies. He explains: "The depiction of Cassidy as a basically harmless and genial individual conflicts with the record. . . . He was . . . misportrayed as being so generous that he was adored by everybody except sheriffs and railroaders."

Yet Butch's sister, Lula Parker Betenson, felt the movie gave an accurate portrayal of her brother. She was consulted during its

35

filming and believed that most of what it depicted was true. She admits, though, that "most of the episodes in the movie involved Elzy Lay instead of the Sundance Kid, but who would go to a movie entitled *Butch Cassidy and Elzy Lay?*"

However, Betenson does not think the movie's ending is true. In its final scene, it shows Butch Cassidy and the Sundance Kid running out into a courtyard, where they will be shot by Bolivian soldiers. The filmmakers used Arthur Chapman's version of what happened to the two outlaws.

But is this really how Butch Cassidy died? To find out, we must first ask two questions: "Is there any evidence that the Bolivian shoot-out actually occurred?" and "Where did Arthur Chapman get his information?" The answers to these questions show why historians must never accept a story without first checking its source.

The Mystery Begins

The mystery of Butch Cassidy's fate began in 1909, when the Pinkerton National Detective Agency lost his trail in Bolivia. Six years earlier, after learning that Butch had changed his name again, Agent Frank P. Dimaio had tracked his movements from New York to South America. Cassidy was now known as Ryan, and the Sundance Kid was Harry E. Place. Etta Place, acting as Harry's wife, was with them.

Ryan's Ranch

Dimaio followed the outlaws' trail to the city of Buenos Aires. There he discovered that they had filed official papers with the Argentine Republic government on April 2, 1902. These papers stated that Place and Ryan had settled on government land within the province of Chubut and owned thirteen hundred sheep, five hundred head of cattle, and thirty-five horses. The two men were asking for the first right to buy the land because they were already improving it.

With this information, Dimaio intended to find the outlaws' homestead. He abandoned this plan when he found out how diffi-cult it was to get there. From Buenos Aires it would take him sev-eral months to reach the seaport nearest the ranch. After that, it would be a fifteen-day ride—*if* the road was even passable. The rainy season had set in, and some people told him a horse would not make it through the mud.

Dimaio contacted the Pinkerton National Detective Agency for advice. His superiors told him to return to the United States, but not before distributing hundreds of wanted posters describing Butch Cassidy and the Sundance Kid.

Dimaio made up these posters in both English and Spanish. He took them to banks, mining supply companies, steamship compa-nies, and police stations. Anyone with any information about the *bandidos Yanquis,* or "Yankee bandits," was asked to notify the Buenos Aires chief of police.

Wanted

Historians disagree about whether Butch saw any of these posters himself. If so, he must have been concerned. He was clearly enjoying his Argentine ranch. He was seen attending local fiestas with Sundance and Etta Place. He had also been struggling to learn Spanish so he could fit in with his neighbors.

Harvey Logan

But if Butch did find out about the wanted posters, it might explain why he abruptly left his ranch in February 1905. Perhaps he realized the law was on his trail, or maybe he was just tired of ranching. In any case, Butch, Sundance, and Etta rode to Rio Gallegos, a town near the southern tip of Argentina. They were accompanied by a man the Pinkerton agency later identified as their old friend Harvey Logan.

In Rio Gallegos the outlaws robbed the Bank of Loudres and Tarapaca. They stole twenty thousand pesos and a box of gold ingots, enough cash to fund their escape from Argentina to Bolivia.

From this point on, historians differ about what happened to the *bandidos Yanquis.* It is uncertain exactly how many robberies they committed and when. In her book, *Butch Cassidy, My Brother,* Lula Parker Betenson explains that just as in the United States, Butch's South American robberies were exploited by other criminals:

> Many outlaws were operating in South America and copied patterns of thefts committed by members of the Wild Bunch in the United States. So once again Butch was given much credit that wasn't due him. Butch realized there was no way out as long as he was alive; he was in too deep to climb out.

Rumors Begin

After a few years, rumors began circulating that Butch and Sundance were dead. According to files still kept in the Pinkerton archives and quoted in *In Search of Butch Cassidy*, on April 5, 1909, an unidentified source, designated informant number 85, from San Francisco told a detective that Cassidy had been killed. The man stated:

> The last I heard from him by letter was from Baggs, Wyo. and he said he wanted Longabaugh to sell his part [of a South American ranching venture], and send him the money as he was going to the northwest territories. I have heard since, from a pretty good source, that . . . he was filled full of holes on the bridge at Green River, Wyo. . . . in the winter of 1905–6.

Other versions of this story soon surfaced. But Butch's friends did not believe he was dead. They had often laughed with Cassidy over rumors that he had been killed someplace or another.

Butch's Argentine Ranch

There is some evidence that Butch Cassidy never intended to leave his Argentine ranch. Perhaps if the Pinkerton agency had not found him, he would have stayed there permanently. This letter, excerpted from Larry Pointer's book, In Search of Butch Cassidy, *shows how much Butch liked his new land. It was written August 10, 1902, to Elzy Lay's mother-in-law in Ashley, Utah.*

"I have never seen a finer grass country, and lots of it hundreds and hundreds of miles that is unsettled, and comparatively unknown, and where I am, it is a good agricultural country, all kind of small grain and vegetables grow without Irrigation. but I am at the foot of the Andes Mountains. and all the land east of here is [prairie] and Deserts, very good for stock, but for farming it would have to be Irrigated, but there is plenty of good land along the Mountain for all the people that will be here for the next hundred years, for I am a long way from Civilation. . . . The climate here is a great deal milder than Ashley Valley. the Summers are beautiful, never as warm as there. And grass knee high every where. and lots of good cold mountain water."

One time Butch even witnessed his own funeral. After a shoot-out near Robbers Roost, a body was misidentified as his. It was buried under a gravestone with Butch's name on it until someone figured out the mistake. In her book, Lula Parker Betenson says her brother enjoyed this incident. She writes:

> When Butch learned through the speedy outlaw grapevine that he had been shot down, he couldn't resist the urge to view his own remains. Hidden in a covered wagon and

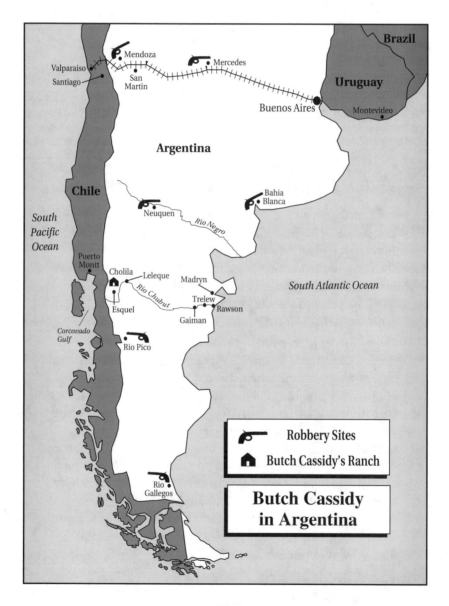

Butch Cassidy in Argentina

Robbery Sites

Butch Cassidy's Ranch

Who Was Etta Place?

There are many different stories about Etta Place's background. In his book, The Outlaw Trail, *Robert Redford says he had a conversation about Sundance's mysterious girlfriend with western writer Edward Abbey and historian Kerry Boren. Boren claimed to have met a son-in-law of Etta Place, who gave him the following information about her:*

"It seems that Etta Place was born circa 1874, the daughter of the Honorable George Capel and the granddaughter of Arthur Algernon Capel, sixth Earl of Essex. Her father was killed before 1892 near Tombstone, Arizona, and Etta was practically raised by the outlaws with whom her father had associated. They even paid for her education. She had been living in the bordello [whorehouse] district of San Antonio, Texas, when Butch Cassidy and his friends, including the Sundance Kid, brought her to Utah where she stayed with a Mormon family for a year or so. She then attended a teacher's college in the East and taught school for about one year in Telluride, Colorado, before joining Butch at Robbers Roost in 1895. . . . She traveled with Butch Cassidy and the Sundance Kid to New York and then Bolivia. The Sundance Kid brought her back to Denver and then returned to South America in 1909. Not much is known about her after that, though there are many versions of the rest of her story. Kerry says he believes she had a long life and had at least one daughter who died in 1971. 'But,' said Ed Abbey, 'no one knows for sure, do they?'"

looking through peepholes, he returned to Price [Utah]. Butch watched the "mourners" and was surprised to see a number of women wiping their eyes. He was touched by such a display of emotion at his passing. Later he told us he had thought it would be a good idea to attend his own funeral just once during his lifetime. He told us, "No, it sure wasn't me. He was better looking."

Butch's Friends Investigate

Consequently, it is no surprise that many of Butch's fellow outlaws ignored the stories of Cassidy's death in South America. They even suspected he had started the rumor himself. Charles Kelly, in his book, *The Outlaw Trail*, says: "Some believed that Cassidy himself had started the story so he could return to the States in safety under another name. He had written some of the boys in Robbers' Roost that things were getting a little too hot in the south and he might return some day."

However, Kelly adds that when Butch did not show up or write any more letters, his friends decided to check out the rumors for themselves. They sent someone to South America to investigate and bring back proof that Butch was dead. Kelly explains:

> It was finally agreed to send a man to South America to ascertain the facts. . . . The emissary [representative] made a trip to the reported scene of Cassidy's last stand, interviewed surviving soldiers who had participated in the battle of San Vicente, obtained photographs taken at the time showing the two dead outlaws, and returned to Utah with his evidence. There seemed to be no question that Cassidy was dead.

But Kelly's sources could not agree on just who had gone to South America to check up on Butch. One woman claimed that Elzy Lay told her it was a man named Burton. Outlaw Matt Warner said it was someone named Walker. Another man said it was bandit Billy Sattell. Some people said that more than one man went. And one witness said that the person in the photographs was not Cassidy at all, but Tom Dilley. Dilley was another outlaw from Robbers Roost who had become one of the *bandidos Yanquis* in South America.

Kelly never saw these photographs himself. There is no proof that they exist or that Butch's friends were telling the truth. Nonetheless, Kelly found them to be credible witnesses.

The Pinkerton Files

Like Butch's friends, the Pinkerton National Detective Agency also heard reports that Butch Cassidy had been killed in South America. A memorandum contained in their archives reveals that Agent Frank Dimaio met with an informant who told him of the outlaw's death. Dimaio said that in 1912 he interviewed Mr. Steele, a traveling agent, in a Detroit restaurant. According to Dimaio, Steele said:

I was in Mercedes [Argentina] last year visiting my trade. When I returned to the hotel one of the guests said to me "Lift up the tarpaulin on the piazza." Upon doing so I saw the bodies of Place, his wife, and Ryan. They had been shot to death while holding up a bank in a nearby village.

However, Dimaio's memorandum about Mr. Steele was dated September 17, 1941. Could it have been influenced by Arthur Chapman's dramatic 1930 account of Butch Cassidy's death? The Pinkerton agency never sent a detective to South America to investigate the matter. Instead, they relied on secondhand stories to conclude that Butch was dead.

Bolivian Police Records

Had the Pinkerton National Detective Agency investigated, they might have learned that Bolivian authorities have no evidence that Butch Cassidy was killed in South America. More importantly, they have no record that a shoot-out ever took place.

The reward poster and descriptions of the Wild Bunch printed and distributed by the Pinkerton agency. The agency never followed up on the reports that Butch and Sundance had been killed in Bolivia.

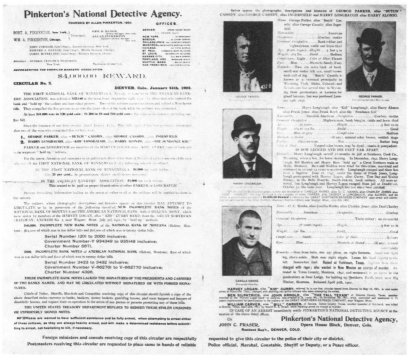

In his book *In Search of Butch Cassidy*, Larry Pointer says that he wrote to the American embassy in Bolivia seeking information about Cassidy's death. On March 18, 1974, Cultural Attaché Graham K. French replied:

> We have attempted to find out from several sources any information that might be available here about these now famous outlaws, and we have drawn blanks everywhere. There appears to be no newspaper accounts of their activities in Bolivia, and [Colonel] Julio Diaz, historian of the Bolivian Army, tells us that he knows of no military action against the two American bandits in Bolivia. They could have been here, he says, but he doubts that the military forces were concerned with them. There are, however, reports that one or both of the two men are buried several kilometers from Tupiza in southern Bolivia.

Mysterious Graves

In the early 1970s, two graves were indeed located near San Vicente, Bolivia. Rumors had long existed that the notorious *bandidos Yanquis* were buried in them. But when the bodies were exhumed and examined, a DNA test proved that they were not Butch Cassidy and the Sundance Kid. So who were they?

No one knows. But South American police records do indicate the existence of two other *bandidos Yanquis*. Their activities were uncovered by Argentine author Justo Piernes in 1970, while he was working on a series of articles about Butch Cassidy for the Buenos Aires newspaper, *Clarin*.

Using Argentine provincial police reports, Piernes learned that Cassidy's old friend Harvey Logan had left Butch's company and joined up with Robert Evans and Williams Wilson, also notorious outlaws from the United States. According to police records dated December 9, 1911, Evans and Wilson were killed in a shoot-out with Argentine authorities.

Piernes found one of the lawmen who killed Evans and Wilson. Piernes interviewed the old man, Don Pedro Penia, and wrote:

> The battle flared when the two outlaws were cornered. Evans unloaded his Winchester and six-shooter at the patrol. He was the first to fall. An officer named Montenegro,

Percy Seibert and Butch Cassidy

Pearl Baker grew up near Robbers Roost and knew a great deal about the outlaws who hid there. In her book, The Wild Bunch at Robbers Roost, *she confirms that Percy Seibert and Butch Cassidy were close friends.*

"Seibert liked Butch, who was using the name of Jim Maxwell [while at the Concordia Tin Mines]. [Seibert] knew all about his employee, and they talked frankly together. Butch told him that he couldn't go straight; as long as he lived, someone would be hounding him. The best strategy was to hit hard and keep moving."

at Penia's side, was shot through the heart by the remaining bandit, Wilson.

Wilson dashed back of a tree, reloading his carbine. "I had discharged three cartridges from my arms," Penia said. "As the bullets went by, I felt I had been caught in the arm. Then I fell, but Wilson also fell, tumbled end over end, and did not get to his horse. He had eight bullets in his body. A lieutenant in the patrol rushed over to the dying Wilson and gave him on the ground the shot of grace.

Penia's story is very similar to Arthur Chapman's. However, it was Evans and Wilson who were killed, not Butch Cassidy and the Sundance Kid.

Who Was Percy Seibert?

All reports of Cassidy's Bolivian shoot-out can be traced to only one source: Chapman's story, or, more correctly, the man who *gave* Chapman his story. This man was Percy Seibert, an American engineer employed by the Concordia Tin Mines in Bolivia.

Sometime in late 1906 or early 1907, Butch and Sundance took a job guarding the payroll of the Concordia Tin Mines. By this time Etta Place had returned to the United States. Some historians believe she had fallen ill and wanted to visit an American hospital.

While working at Concordia, Butch met Percy Seibert. Seibert had originally come to Bolivia to help with the planning of the proposed Bolivian railway. However, he had been fired for not getting

Were reports of Cassidy's death concocted by his friends to keep the Pinkerton agency off his trail?

along with his supervisor. He was soon hired by the Concordia Tin Mines, where he and Butch quickly became friends.

In his book, *In Search of Butch Cassidy*, Larry Pointer quotes a letter written by Seibert to someone named Elizabeth on January 15, 1964. In it Seibert describes his relationship with Butch Cassidy. He writes:

> Butch Cassidy was an agreeable and pleasant person, a grandson of an elder of the Mormon Church. He took well with the ladies and as soon as he arrived in a village he made friends with the little urchins and usually had some candy to give them. When he visited me he enjoyed hearing the gramophone records, as I had a large selection of choice music. He allowed no other bandits to interfere with my camp and told them when they needed an animal shod or they needed a meal I would take care of them, but that they should move on and keep their backs toward my

camp and not give it the reputation of being a bandit's hangout. When he last visited me, he asked me a couple of times if I was sure he did not owe our [company] store anything more than the six or eight dollars I told him of and which he immediately paid.

. . . [Butch and Sundance] said that after a holdup or two, they had to continue as the Pinkertons, U.S. Cavalry and Bankers Association and Railroad detectives were constantly on their trail. I never had the slightest trouble getting along with them. Cassidy purchased cattle and mules for us and always was scrupulously honest as far as we were concerned. He went to a mining camp owned by a pair of wealthy Scotchmen, to get the lay-of-the-land and to learn when their payroll remittances would arrive so as to pick it up. They gave him a job as a night watchman and told him they really needed no one, but wanted to give him a chance to make a little money so he could continue prospecting for mines, as on applying for work he told them he was a prospector and had run out of money and supplies. They told him the meal hours, told him the sideboard had a supply of whiskey, . . . water, gin, and beer and whenever he felt like a drink to help himself. He told me after, that he had not the heart to hold up people who treated him so kindly.

Clearly Percy Seibert admired Butch Cassidy—and Seibert was the sole source for Arthur Chapman's story. With no other witnesses to the event, his description of the Bolivian shoot-out is suspect. Could he have been lying?

Rumors of Butch's Death Exaggerated

Lula Parker Betenson says yes, and she claims to know why. Betenson says that Seibert wanted to help Butch. She says that in 1925 Butch told her Seibert owed him a favor. Betenson quotes her brother as saying:

I heard they got Percy Seibert from the Concordia Tin Mines to identify a couple of bodies as Butch Cassidy and the Sundance Kid all right. I wondered why Mr. Seibert did that. Then it dawned on me that he would know this was

the only way we could go straight. I'd been close to Seibert—we'd talked a lot, and he knew how sick of the [outlaw]
life I was. He knew I'd be hounded as long as I lived. Well,
I'm sure he saw this as a way for me to bury my past along
with somebody else's body so I could start over. I'd saved
his and [Concordia manager] Mr. Glass's lives on a couple
of occasions, and I guess he figured this was how he could
pay me back.

If Betenson is correct, then Butch Cassidy did not die in Bolivia.
Instead he simply assumed a new identity after 1909. He then al-
lowed everyone to *think* he was dead. He had already proven himself to be a master at escape, so it is easy to imagine that he
outwitted the Pinkertons one more time.

But who did he become? Are there any clues regarding his new
identity? The answers to these questions are perhaps the most interesting aspect of the Butch Cassidy mystery.

 3 *Exploring Other Identities*

For six years after the publication of Arthur Chapman's article, most people were certain that Butch Cassidy had been killed in South America. Then, in 1936, a rumor began to spread that one or two years earlier, Butch had shown up in the town of Lander, Wyoming, to visit some old friends.

Mart T. Christensen, treasurer of Wyoming, became interested in these rumors. Christensen had been put in charge of the Wyoming Writers Project, a research project funded by the federal government. One of the goals of the Writers Project was to document the history of Wyoming. Christensen felt that the story of Butch Cassidy was an important part of Wyoming's past.

There were two other reasons he was interested in Butch Cassidy. Both of them were personal. Christensen had grown up in Baggs, Wyoming, at a time when the town was often visited by the

Never Ask Questions

Arthur Ekker, rancher and lifetime resident of the Robbers Roost area, offers one explanation for why Butch's whereabouts remained secret for so long. In Robert Redford's book, The Outlaw Trail, *Ekker says:*

"When I was a kid we were told never to ask questions when a stranger came to town. Agreement was no one would talk. We kids never knew nothin'. Our folks knew but they'd never say. Lotsa folk round these parts believe [Butch Cassidy] never died in Bolivia. I never saw him, but a fella named Whiting from over to Hanksville who used to take supplies out here to the Roost for Butch, claimed he seen him in the twenties."

well-liked Butch and his Wild Bunch. In addition, in 1909 Mart Christensen's fiancée, Mary Calvert, had run off to marry Butch's friend Elzy Lay, who had been released from prison three years earlier. Christensen felt as though Butch Cassidy had always been a part of his life.

In July 1936 William G. Johnson, register of the U.S. Land Office, learned of Christensen's interest in Butch Cassidy. Johnson, who had once lived in Lander, Wyoming, had important information about the outlaw. He wrote:

> During the summer of 1935, Butch Cassidy bought [food and supplies] from Harry Baldwin, pioneer merchant at Lander. He then had 2 Lander men deliver him somewhere in the Indian Reservation. At a certain point, Butch dismissed his companions and proceeded alone. Soon thereafter [he] departed for his home in Seattle, Wash.

On August 8, 1936, Wyoming historian Tacetta B. Walker sent similar information to Christensen. She said that many of Butch's old friends in Lander claimed to have seen him in 1934, fifteen years after his supposed death in South America. She said they had been well acquainted with the outlaw and could not have been mistaken. Walker wrote:

> One old timer who roomed with [Butch Cassidy] claimed he recognized him by a scar on his head. Another one told me that Cassidy did not tell him he was Butch Cassidy until he told him he knew him. Then [Cassidy] told him a story that only he, Butch Cassidy, and one other knew. The third party was dead so that left only Cassidy and himself as knowing the story.

Charles Kelly's Attitude

Christensen decided to send staff members from his Writers Project to interview the citizens of Lander, Wyoming. They reported more stories regarding Butch Cassidy's visit to their town. Christensen believed these stories without doubt.

Then Tacetta Walker told him about Charles Kelly, who was just in the process of writing his book, *The Outlaw Trail*. Walker had learned that Kelly planned to say that Butch Cassidy died in Bolivia. When Christensen heard this he decided to contact the author.

The main street of Lander, Wyoming, in 1930, about the time Cassidy was supposed to have shown up to visit friends—years after he was reported dead.

Christensen told Kelly his facts were wrong. He suggested that Kelly examine the interviews conducted by the Wyoming Writers Project. Kelly responded by saying that these stories were unimportant. The author felt that Christensen's witnesses were unreliable, in part because of their advanced ages.

This made Christensen angry. He wrote the author another letter on June 19, 1937. Taken from Pointer's *In Search of Butch Cassidy*, the letter stated:

> I will not burden you with the details of Butch Cassidy's visit [to Wyoming] in the summer of 1934 but it is enough to relate that an old friend of Cassidy's by the name of Hank Boedeker, 78, but very alert and active for his age, spent the best part of a day with Butch Cassidy on that occasion. It is common knowledge in that entire vicinity that Butch Cassidy did visit there during 1934 and the purpose of his visit. He talked to Harry Baldwin, Wyoming

Many People Saw Him

In her book, Butch Cassidy, My Brother, *Lula Parker Betenson offers the testimony of many people who were certain that Butch Cassidy returned from South America. One such person was Mrs. Margaret Simpson from Dubois, Wyoming. Years earlier Butch had worked on her husband's ranch and had been like a son to her. Betenson says:*

"[Margaret] never saw him after he was supposed to have returned from South America, but she knew Will Simpson [the prosecuting attorney who had sent Butch to the Wyoming State Penitentiary] caught a glimpse of him one day. Will stayed under cover, fearing reprisal."

merchant, who sold him a bill of grub [supply of food] and to Ed Farlow, a former mayor of Lander, who knew him during his early days. Now, if I were interested enough in the life of Butch Cassidy to write a book I would forthwith visit Hank Boedeker, Ed Farlow, and Harry Baldwin in Lander. . . . It will explode all the "bunk" [nonsense] put out by the several writers who finish the life of Cassidy in South America with such dramatics.

. . . It would be preposterous to assert to any of the people I have named that they are mistaken.

Reluctantly, Charles Kelly decided to interview the old-timers of Lander. But even though he heard the same stories about Butch Cassidy's visit there, he still dismissed them. To Kelly, none of these rumors was as reliable as Arthur Chapman's story. However, he does acknowledge that there is a "bare possibility" these rumors are true.

Kelly's attitude might have been influenced by stories about another outlaw. Five years prior to the publication of *The Outlaw Trail*, an eighty-seven-year-old man falsely claimed he was Jesse James. Like Cassidy, James was a notorious bank and train robber whose death has always been controversial. For years after his death on April 3, 1882, many people believed that James had not really been killed by Robert Ford, a member of his gang. Rumors circulated that the body in James's grave was not his. However, recently that body was exhumed, and scientists have tentatively identified it as that of Jesse James.

Many More Rumors

In *The Outlaw Trail,* Kelly compares the rumors about Jesse James with those about Butch Cassidy. He then briefly lists alternate versions of what might have happened to Butch, beginning with the statement of a former lawman. Kelly reports: "Robert Hildebrand, an old post-office detective who says he knew Cassidy personally, declares the outlaw returned to Brown's Hole after he was reported killed, and died not many years ago."

Kelly next mentions a story that Butch went to his family home in Circleville, Utah, in 1905. His mother had just died, and Butch supposedly wanted to view her body. This event would have occurred before Butch's Bolivian shoot-out, but it is significant be-

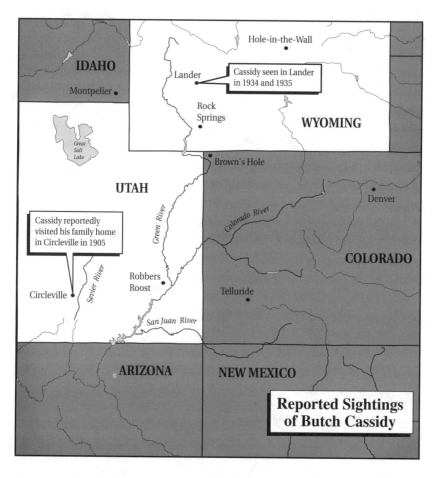

Reported Sightings of Butch Cassidy

cause it places him in the United States when he was supposed to have been in South America. Kelly explains:

> [Butch] is said to have arrived in the night and left during the following night. Friends of Mrs. Parker were not allowed to enter the house where the body lay during that day, a strange procedure in southern Utah, where neighbors always offer their services on such occasions. Mrs. Ann Campbell Parker died on May 1, 1905, three years after her outlaw son is said to have left the United States.

However, Lula Parker Betenson disputes this account. She says it is another example of misinformation about her brother, and she faults historians like Kelly for perpetuating such falsehoods. In *Butch Cassidy, My Brother*, she writes:

> A number of writers have claimed my brother returned for Mother's funeral. One author whom I know personally leaves his readers with the impression that I told him my mother lay in state in Circleville for twenty-four hours with no visitors and that Butch paid his respects that night. This is not true. We had an almost continuous flow of friends and relatives until time for the funeral on May 5. Butch, in South America, did not even know of Mother's death, and he certainly did not come.

Charles Kelly mentions several more rumors about Butch Cassidy. He tells of one story involving Butch's former partner, Matt Warner:

> John Wesley Warf says that one day in Price [Utah], about 1915, he stepped into Matt Warner's saloon, where he observed a man sitting with his back to the wall. Warner and Warf were intimately acquainted. "Know who that is?" asked Matt in a whisper. "No," Warf replied, "I don't recognize him." "That's Butch Cassidy. He's staying with me for a while; but keep it under your hat." But Matt was always a great joker.

Cassidy in Mexico?

Kelly similarly dismisses two stories that have Butch Cassidy living out his life in Mexico. He attributes them to misunderstandings. He says:

Various stories circulating in Utah are to the effect that Cassidy is still living in Mexico. One such is told by Henry Bowman, of Cedar City, Utah. It seems that Bowman, a member of the Mormon colony in Mexico, was captured by a band of Pancho Villa's soldiers during the revolution and had been lined up against a wall to be shot. As a last resort, Bowman pleaded with the officer in charge to allow him to speak with his friend, Cassidy, before the execution. Cassidy had been a resident of those parts for many years and was well known to the officer, so the request was granted. A messenger was sent and Cassidy arrived in haste. When he saw Bowman he protested the boy's innocence of any connection with the Federals, vouched for his honesty, and agreed to be responsible for his future actions. The officer was convinced and Bowman was freed, returning to Utah shortly afterward. The incident is undoubtedly true. But, according to Jim Marshall, an old-timer who knew both, the man who saved Bowman's life was Mike Cassidy, the old southern Utah bandit whose name was taken by George LeRoy Parker. Mike, says Marshall, once returned to his old haunts in Utah, dressed in broadcloth and a high silk hat. The two men met in the little store at Molan. Mike winked at Marshall and nodded to meet him outside. "You won't give me away, will you, Jim?" asked Mike. "I'm just back for a short visit." Marshall promised. Mike Cassidy then left the country, but letters were received from him later stating he had married a woman with property in Mexico and was living the life of a hidalgo [Spanish nobleman]. That man, says Marshall, is the Cassidy who saved Bowman's life. And Jim ought to know.

Another story comes from Harry Ogden, who as a boy met Cassidy several times in Robbers Roost. "In 1923," says Ogden, "I was working on the international ditch just over the Mexican border. In a little Mexican saloon where the men gambled on pay days, I met Cassidy dealing in one of the games. He called me to one side and cautioned me not to mention his old name. He recalled the time we had traded horses and seemed anxious to hear all the news of his family and friends in Utah. He said he was then living on an island just off the coast. It was later reported that he had died there in 1932."

The Idaho-Washington Connection

However, Kelly does not discount two reports of Cassidy's living in Idaho. In his book, *The Outlaw Trail,* he merely reports them without comment. He says:

Another story generally believed by many was told by the late Anthony Ivins, first counselor to the president of the Mormon church, an old-time westerner who knew Cassidy as a boy. Mr. Ivins asserted positively that Cassidy was still living in Idaho under an assumed name which he felt under obligation of friendship not to reveal. The same story is told by an old Salt Lake barber who was raised in Circleville.

The Idaho stories are important because they place Butch Cassidy near Spokane, Washington. Spokane is only a few miles from the Idaho-Washington border. It is also the city where Lula Parker Betenson says her brother lived out his remaining years after leaving South America. In an interview with the *Billings Gazette* on November 8, 1970, she said: "The law thought he was dead and he was happy to leave it that way. He made us promise not to tell anyone that he was alive. And we never did. It was the tightest family secret. He died peacefully in Spokane in 1937."

Former friends of Butch also place him in Washington State. In his book, *In Search of Butch Cassidy,* Larry Pointer states: "Although early reports as to his residence varied from Seattle to Spokane, there had emerged a consistent mention of Spokane."

Charles Kelly agrees that this was the most common location given for Butch Cassidy's whereabouts. In *The Outlaw Trail* he says:

In compiling her . . . book, *Early Days in Wyoming,* Tacetta B. Walker was told by several old-timers near Lander that Butch Cassidy had been in that vicinity as late as 1934, had stayed several months, and had later gone to Spokane, where he was still living in 1937. This story, identical in detail, came to me from several different sources, and the evidence seemed thoroughly convincing.

Good Guys Versus Bad Guys

In his book, The Outlaw Trail, *Robert Redford says that Butch Cassidy was not necessarily a "bad guy" just because he robbed banks. He believes that the outlaws of Butch's time were different from modern criminals.*

"We have an abiding impression of the [Old West] outlaw as a low-life renegade, a violent fool who lived off luck and the gun. We view him as one of society's misbegotten who had to be hunted down like an animal by morally superior men in white hats. But it was not so. In truth, the line between the 'good guy' and the 'bad guy' in the West was often blurred, and many of the outlaws, in spite of their errant and often violent natures, were men of extraordinary skill and cunning, who by comparison made the lawmen look pathetic."

The people who told this story said that Butch was using a new name in Spokane. Many of them refused to reveal it. However, several others gave away the secret. In a letter to Charles Kelly dated August 1, 1936, Tacetta Walker said that one old-timer from Lander told her that "he believed Cassidy was going by the name of Bill Phillips in Spokane, Washington. . . . And from what they say, he would probably not admit being Cassidy."

William G. Johnson from the U.S. Land Office agreed. In a 1936 memo to Wyoming treasurer Mart Christensen, quoted in *In Search of Butch Cassidy,* he said that Butch "is known as William Phillips. He now has cancer of the stomach and is not expected to live much longer."

In his June 19, 1937, letter to Charles Kelly, Christensen also mentioned Phillips. He wrote: "George LeRoy Parker, alias Butch Cassidy—now known as William Phillips, in the state of Washington—was alive six months ago and resides in Spokane."

"The Real Butch Cassidy"

One month after Christensen wrote to Kelly, William Phillips was dead. Despite reports of his poor health, no one had rushed to interview him—particularly not Charles Kelly, who said he was not interested in the man.

Was William Phillips (pictured) the real Butch Cassidy? Several of his friends and associates reported that he was Cassidy.

Then in September 1937 a Wyoming newspaper article made a bold statement about William Phillips. It reported that he had died of rectal cancer on July 20, 1937, and called him "the real Butch Cassidy." Charles Kelly was astonished.

Kelly believed this connection between Cassidy and Phillips was the result of an unverified claim. In *The Outlaw Trail*, he wrote:

> Notice of his death was given to the papers by a man in Lander who claimed to have ridden with Butch Cassidy in early days and couldn't possibly be fooled by a pretender. This old friend did not attempt to explain how Butch had survived the battle of San Vicente [Bolivia], but he stated positively that William Phillips of Spokane was the real Butch Cassidy and that he finally died in July, 1937.

Now that William Phillips was no longer alive to be interviewed, Charles Kelly eagerly sought information about him. He wrote to the Washington State Bureau of Vital Statistics to obtain the man's death certificate. In *The Outlaw Trail* Kelly says: "The statements therein prove positively that Phillips was not Cassidy." Kelly bases his opinion on the fact that the certificate says Phillips was born not in Utah, but in Michigan.

However, while conducting research for *In Search of Butch Cassidy*, Larry Pointer discovered that the certificate's information about William Phillips's birth was false. He says:

> Where Charles Kelly's research ended, ours had to begin. William Phillips' death record placed his birth as June 22, 1865, in Michigan. His father was listed as L. J. Phillips; his mother's maiden name as Celia Mudge. Records in the Spokane Elks and Masonic lodges further listed his birthplace as Sandusky, Michigan, and his father's name as Laddie J. Phillips.
>
> Research in Michigan census records failed to produce a Laddie J. Phillips. Sandusky records did show a Celia Mudge, born in Sanilac County on November 19, 1852, but she would have been twelve years old in 1865, the year of Phillips' listed birth date. At age twenty-two, in February 1875, Celia Mudge was married at Minden, Michigan, to Hezakiah Snell. The couple's descendents know little of their grandparents and nothing of William Phillips.

William Phillips's home in Spokane, Washington. Could the real Butch Cassidy have lived out his last days in a quiet, small town?

Sandusky, Michigan, was not formed until 1870, and birth certificates were not issued in Sanilac County until 1867. There is, then, no documentation of the birth of "William Thadeus Phillips."

Larry Pointer also says that the age listed on Phillips's death certificate increases the possibility that Phillips was Cassidy, as does the cause of death. He states: "His age, listed as seventy-two on the death certificate, would have been comparable to that of the outlaw, and William G. Johnson's note [to Mart Christensen] that Phillips had cancer of the stomach is remarkably similar to the attending physician's statement of cause of death as cancer of the rectum."

But Charles Kelly was not impressed by such details. He decided that William Phillips's widow, Gertrude Phillips would know the truth. He wrote to her for information about her husband's life.

On October 4, 1938, Mrs. Phillips replied. The information she gave Charles Kelly about William Phillips offers some interesting clues regarding the true identity of Butch Cassidy.

4 Who Was William T. Phillips?

When William T. Phillips's widow wrote to Charles Kelly about her husband's life, her story proved to have some puzzling aspects. She said that Phillips had once ridden with Butch Cassidy, yet there is no record that Cassidy ever had such a companion.

More importantly, the facts she gave about this association and about her husband's life in general seemed intentionally vague. In a passage quoted in *In Search of Butch Cassidy* she wrote:

> It came to my mind last eve. that at least I could do as you suggested and give you a brief outline of Mr. Phillips' life; tho' am afraid there will be little in it of interest to you, because I am unable to give you an account of the part of it in which you, naturally are most interested, viz. [namely], the few years in which he knew and rode the range with Cassidy.
>
> Wm. T. Phillips was born and raised in an eastern state until he reached the age of 14 years; at which time (owing to dime novel influence) he ran away and headed for the Black Hills, where he was greatly disillusioned in regard to many things, as he was bound to be; after a few months of seeing his small hoard dwindle away, and failing to find work because of his youth and inability to convince anyone he could hold down a man's job, he became homesick and started out to make his way back home.
>
> It was in the fall of the year, and he finally succeeded in obtaining work on a ranch during harvest, and (tho I've heard him tell about it), I'm not sure just where that was, but in the corn belt, for he often laughed at the speed he acquired in husking corn. He enjoyed the people with whom he found himself, and stayed till the following Spring, when,

having survived his homesickness, decided to stay a while longer in the west, and again headed for the Black Hills. It was after that, of course, that he fell in with Cassidy; but not having it all in detail, I can not give you much satisfaction as to how it all came about, except that it was at the time of the Johnson County War, and I've heard him express himself as being in sympathy with the "little fellows" instead of the stock association. He thought he knew Cassidy very, very well; and considered he was much more sinned against than sinning. As to just how long he was associated with him I am unable to say, for my memory is none to [*sic*] good as to dates, etc. and I haven't that all in detail, as I have his account of Cassidy, in which he makes no mention of himself.

Later he did mural decorating in New York City for two or three years; at one time had a machine shop in Des Moines, Iowa, for about seven or eight years. After he and I were married, we lived in Arizona for a year; came to Spokane, and have been here ever since, until his death last year.

William Phillips's wife said he told her stories about riding with the Wild Bunch—although no Phillips (pictured) was ever known to have ridden with the group.

That, in brief, is the story of my husband. I wrote you that we each knew Cassidy; so we did; I knew his family, but I can tell you little, I think that you do not already know; however both Mr. Phillips and myself came originally from the east; *not the middle west.*

Money for Information?

Charles Kelly printed an extremely brief version of Mrs. Phillips's letter in his book, *The Outlaw Trail.* He made no comments about it. He merely followed it with this paragraph about William Phillips:

> Phillips, representing himself as Cassidy, searched the mountains near Fort Washakie [Wyoming] with Bill Boyd for $70,000 supposed to have been buried there by Butch. He met Hank Boedeker of Dubois [Wyoming], who knew Cassidy well in the old days, but was not recognized as an impostor. He also fooled several old-timers in the vicinity of Lander and Wilcox, who swore they could not be mistaken.

Kelly gives no source for this information. He says nothing more about William T. Phillips. He also leaves out the final comments in Mrs. Phillips's letter. In a quote taken from *In Search of Butch Cassidy* she wrote:

> So I'm afraid there is little of interest that I can acquaint you with, concerning the western experiences, tho' I wish I could, for I would very much like to figure out some way whereby I could better myself financially; the depression of '29 is responsible for my present circumstances; we have a son who is not old enough yet to become established in business; and present conditions are not too favorable for young fellows of his age; however, we hope to weather through, and if war does not yet break out, we, as others, have a better chance.

Could Mrs. Phillips have been suggesting that she needed financial compensation for her story? Was this paragraph a subtle hint for Charles Kelly to send her money in exchange for information?

William R. Phillips, the adopted son of Gertrude and William T. Phillips, does not think so. He says his father was indeed Butch

Cassidy. But he believes his mother did not say so because she did not want to become famous. Larry Pointer, in his book *In Search of Butch Cassidy*, explains:

> In Spokane William R. Phillips told us the fact that his father was Butch Cassidy was accepted in their home. He had never been told otherwise, by either William or Gertrude Phillips. It was however, a well-guarded family secret. The younger Phillips, adopted by the couple shortly after his birth in 1919, today is puzzled at his father's national fame. When Charles Kelly wrote his mother, he remembers that she purposely camouflaged her husband's background: "She just didn't want the notoriety."

Digging Deeper

Larry Pointer has examined Mrs. Phillips's letter to Charles Kelly very carefully. In doing so he has discovered several problems with it. He reveals:

> In her letter to Charles Kelly, [Mrs. Phillips] said they had lived in Arizona for a year before moving to Spokane, where city directories first listed the couple in 1911. Gertrude Phillips said that previous to their marriage her husband "did mural decorating in New York City for two or three years; at one time had a machine shop in Des Moines, Iowa, for about seven or eight years."
>
> Neither Des Moines nor New York City records support Mrs. Phillips' contention. Before May 14, 1908, the date of his marriage to Gertrude Livesay in Adrian, Michigan, there is no documentary evidence William T. Phillips ever existed.
>
> In other words, Pointer could find no proof that any of the information

William Phillips

Mrs. Phillips wrote about her husband was true. Her story is as un-substantiated as Arthur Chapman's Bolivian shoot-out. Could she have been concealing information, as her son suggested?

To find out, Pointer interviewed other people who had known William Phillips. One woman, Blanche Lundstrom Glasgow, had a particularly interesting story to tell. Blanche was the widow of Bill Lundstrom, who had known Butch Cassidy. Pointer discovered that:

> Bill Lundstrom had known Phillips as Butch Cassidy during the 1890s in Wyoming and Montana, where Lundstrom was a bartender. His wife Blanche met Phillips in Spokane through her husband in 1914. Once Phillips became acquainted with her, Blanche said he took her into his confidence. She recalled the parties they attended and the evenings she and Bill Lundstrom spent listening to Phillips talk of his outlaw days as Butch Cassidy. He told of robbing banks and trains, of hiding with the Indians to evade pursuing posses, and of his adventures in South America.

> Only a few of Phillips' inner circle of friends heard him tell of his outlaw past. He never seemed to talk about it around [his wife] Gertrude, Blanche recalled. She and her husband kept it secret, "because we just figured he never wanted it told. He told it to us in secret."

"The Bandit Invincible"

Blanche Glasgow provided another important link between Butch Cassidy and William T. Phillips: a manuscript by Phillips entitled "The Bandit Invincible." Phillips's widow was referring to this manuscript when she wrote to Charles Kelly, "I have his account of Cassidy, in which he makes no mention of himself." It relates the story of Butch Cassidy's life in a third-person narrative.

At the beginning of "The Bandit Invincible," which is quoted at length in Pointer's book, Phillips says that not everything in his manuscript is true. He explains: "As all the characters depicted in this book have taken an actual part, I find it essential to substitute some of the real names of both persons and places which I shall mention. Also, some places of the holdups have been changed."

Nonetheless, it is a revealing document. William T. Phillips first began to write "The Bandit Invincible" by hand after returning from

"Avoid Forming a Habit"

If "The Bandit Invincible" is a true story, then William Phillips's remarks, quoted in Pointer's book, about how Butch Cassidy escaped capture are important. Phillips writes:

"Habit is one of the most Potent factors which aid in the capture of crimnals. realizing this, Butch has always made it a Point to avoid forming a habit of any sort. He changed his walk, the combing of his hair, how he wore his hat and the style of his clothes. He often noticed that a change of hats was one of the most effective disguises a man could affect and he never failed to make use of it. no matter how rediculous a certain hat made him look. he would unhesitatingly make the change.

Cassidy never over estimated his own ability, nor under estimated the ability of his pursuers, but, he at all times applied very natural Psychology in all his actions, and avoided all the things the other fellow would most naturally conclude that he would also. So there was practically no way of getting a line on him unless one was to meet him face to face, and then very few would recognize him, unless they had been quite well acquainted with him."

a trip to Wyoming in 1934—the same year the old-timers there said they had seen Butch Cassidy. Phillips had told his wife he was going on a business trip to South America. Instead he went to revisit places from his youth. The preface to his manuscript reads:

Back to old Wyoming where I roamed in the days of [yore],
Searching for the faces of my pals, of long ago.
Gone, are they, forever, from the mountain and the dales;
Ne'er, again I'll see them, midst the hills I love so well.

Larry Pointer says that the idea for the manuscript came from Ellen Harris, a friend of Phillips's from Spokane. Harris knew that William T. Phillips was Butch Cassidy, and she felt he should write down the true story of his life. Her son Ben, a Hollywood actor and prop man, agreed to market the book.

However, once he read the story, Ben refused to help get the manuscript published. He said that no one would believe any western outlaw would actually end up in South America. Phillips tried to sell the story to a few magazines, but they rejected it. Eventually he abandoned the manuscript, and his handwritten pages were destroyed.

Fortunately, Blanche Lundstrom Glasgow had made her own copy. She, her daughters, and her sister had carefully written it down from the original manuscript. They used four separate notebooks. Sometimes they preserved the spelling and capitalization mistakes of the original, which also appear here. Other times it appears they made corrections. When they were finished, they had approximately 188 pages of material.

"The Bandit Invincible" began with a foreword that stated:

> Many descriptions have been written of "Butch" Cassidy by various men, some of which were fairly accurate, but as a whole, seemed more or less conjectures.

Did Butch Cassidy write an autobiography called "The Bandit Invincible," in which he disguised himself by writing in the third person?

It has been my pleasure to have known "Butch" Cassidy since his early boyhood, and I am happy to say, that I have never known a more courageous and kinder hearted man in my life time. his reputation for varacity and intigrity in all his dealings, aside from holdups, is unquestioned. I have known him on several occasions to suffer both cold and hunger, in order to help some one whom he thought needed food and shelter more than he. The mystery of "Butch's" evasion of capture for so many years is very simple, "Friends." He had many friends in all walks of life. I knew of only one man, either in North or South of America, who might have been any enemy to him and eaven he respected his truthfulness. . . .

Cassidy did not rob for the lust of gain, nor was it his natural trend. He had as he thought, every good reason for his first holdup, and after the first, there was no place to stop.

i cannot feel he was entirely a victim of circumstances; and that, in a way he was goaded on to become the most dreaded, most hunted and surely the most illusive outlaw that either North or South America have had to contend with as yet.

Justifying His Life

After studying "The Bandit Invincible," Larry Pointer made some conclusions about the man who wrote the manuscript. He noted that "over half of his manuscript is devoted to details of Butch Cassidy's deeds of human kindness and to rationalization of his outlaw career."

Phillips wrote the manuscript at a time when he was already dying of cancer. Pointer believes this is a significant clue to the reason Phillips wrote "The Bandit Invincible." He says:

Viewing his certain death, Phillips had to believe his life was not lived in vain. He had to justify his existence. He had to demonstrate how his sometimes nefarious [wicked] activities had tried to make a point. . . . In short, "The Bandit Invincible" is the last testament of a man who did wrong, who knew he did wrong, and who felt a need to tell others why he did wrong. It was Butch Cassidy's peace with his Maker.

Sundance and Etta

The following excerpt from "The Bandit Invincible" and quoted in the Pointer book discusses the relationship between the Sundance Kid and Etta Place. Here and elsewhere in his manuscript, Phillips refers to Etta as Betty Price. He calls Sundance Dick Maxwell—an interesting detail, considering that Cassidy was known as Maxwell while at the Concordia Tin Mines.

"Maxwell had a sweet heart who always seemed to know of his whereabouts and would occationally pay him a visit, but never for any length of time. She was a smart woman and beautiful to look at. What her early history was no one knew, she apparently loved Maxwell dearly, but was not the mushy type.

Maxwell was much in love with Betty Price and was extreamaly jealous in his respect for her. Unfortunate was any man who intentionally, or otherwise passed an disperoging remark about Betty in his presence. At one time he knocked a man cold for simply remarking that he'd give half his interest in heaven for that woman. . . .

Betty was a true match for Dick Maxwell. She at all times looked and carried herself like a lady attending to her own business and showed no interest in any one but Maxwell. When they first met I do not know, neither did I know whether they were married or not. Of one thing I am certain, they were truly devoted all through the years I knew them in the United States and South America."

Pointer felt that this attitude added credibility to the Phillips manuscript. However, he did not rely on emotion when studying "The Bandit Invincible." He painstakingly checked out all the dates, places, and other details mentioned in the story.

Little-Known Facts

What Pointer found convinced him that William T. Phillips really was Butch Cassidy. Many of the details Phillips gave in his manuscript were not common knowledge. They had not been published in newspaper accounts about Butch's robberies, nor did most people know about them. In his book, *In Search of Butch Cassidy,* Pointer says:

> Careful scrutiny has proven the Phillips' narrative often to bear more truth than recorded history itself. This manuscript written in 1934 described people and places at the turn of the century with an accuracy attainable only through firsthand experience. Only a person who had actually been in the places described and had known the people discussed would have been able to provide such intimate detail. What discrepancies occur can be attributed either to distortions of memory or to Phillips' qualifying preface in protection of those who took an actual part.

Pointer gives several examples that prove Phillips was writing from firsthand knowledge. In one instance, his manuscript mentions "Lone Bear's village, a little above the Big Bend" of Wind River in Fremont County, Wyoming. Pointer discovered that Lone Bear had indeed been a real person—an Arapaho who at one time had been chief of his tribe. Lone Bear had died in 1920, fourteen years before Phillips began writing "The Bandit Invincible."

Pointer found Lone Bear's son, Vincent Brown, who verified that Lone Bear's village once stood in the exact location William Phillips described. The town of Riverton, Wyoming, had been built on that site in 1906. Therefore, as Pointer concludes, "Only a person who had visited Lone Bear's village before [1906] could have described the Arapaho camp."

In another instance, Phillips mentions Sheriff Orson Grimmett and his deputy Jim Baldwin. He says that besides being a sheriff, Grimmett owned a saloon in Lander, Wyoming. After much research, Pointer discovered that this information was also accurate. Sheriff Orson Grimmett served as county sheriff from 1895 to 1897 and again from 1899 to 1901. The "Free Silver Saloon, Grimmett and Davis proprietors" is listed in the 1896 Lander city directory. In addition, Pointer found a photograph of Grimmett and Deputy Baldwin standing in a Lander saloon.

Another South American Shoot-Out

Such verifiable details suggest that "The Bandit Invincible" is a true story. But if it is, does that necessarily mean William Phillips was Butch Cassidy? Or, as Phillips himself stated at the beginning of his manuscript, had he merely been Cassidy's constant companion?

"The Bandit Invincible" describes Butch Cassidy's life not only in the United States, but in South America. Larry Pointer has studied the dates, times, and places mentioned in the South American portion of the manuscript. Using newspaper accounts and Cassidy's own letters, he believes he can place the outlaw in the locations mentioned by Phillips.

The Sundance Kid and girlfriend, Etta Place. According to "The Bandit Invincible," Sundance died in Bolivia.

Yet there is no evidence that a man named William Phillips accompanied Butch, Sundance, and Etta to South America. There is also no record of William Phillips having participated in any Bolivian robberies. If Phillips was in South America, no one—not even the Pinkerton National Detective Agency—knew he was there.

But perhaps Phillips was not in South America with Cassidy. Perhaps Butch had simply told him what happened there. Cassidy might have visited Phillips the same way he visited his old friends in Lander, Wyoming.

"The Bandit Invincible" supports this possibility. In the manuscript, William Phillips says Butch Cassidy decided that somehow he was going to find a way to leave South America. He wanted to return to the United States and marry a girlfriend there. Phillips writes:

> Cassidy was of a Verry determined disposition and when an Idea or desire became rooted in his mind he never abanded it and nothing but death could force him from the hope, that some day some how he could leave the [outlaw] life, with the women he so dearly loved in the far off united states. He could find no definate plan, but the Idea rangled [festered] in [him] to accept the first opportunity that presented it self.

Phillips says that Butch's opportunity came when something went wrong during a train robbery. Butch, Sundance (whom Phillips calls Maxwell), and two other men named Billings and Hains had just begun to board the train when Bolivian soldiers appeared and started shooting. This shoot-out bore many similarities to Arthur Chapman's story of Butch's death. But Phillips's version has a different outcome. He writes:

> A commotion was heard at the rear of the train beyond the curve and before [Butch and his men] realized what was hapening a detachmint of Bolivian cavalry made its apearence around the curve and opened fire on them. The Bandits were suprised and hurried to shelter behind some large boilders which lay at the mouth of the Gorge, before it begin to rain bullets and spattered against the rocks from all directions.
>
> Billings was wounded in the first atact but the bandits killed eleven soldiers. and 7 wounded. Billings was finaly

The Sundance Kid and Kid Curry

*In these two passages from "The Bandit Invincible,"
quoted in Pointer's book, William Phillips describes the
personalities of the Sundance Kid, whom he calls Dick
Maxwell, and Kid Curry.*

"Dick Maxwell was a man about Butchs size and build but
was slightly darker than Butch. He like Butch was quick as a
steal trap in his movements and a dead shot.

Maxwell was a natural born gentle man and had all the
earmarks of one. Always emaculate in appearance and the
attitude of the perfect gentle man. He like Cassidy was the
champion of the under dog. . . . Maxwell was not what one
would call sullen, but he was Verry reserved & dispositioned
to be distant except with his Verry closest friends and there
were times when he held himself aloof from them. he was
quick and active with a six shooter and if in a fit of temper or
attracted he could shoot on the instant.

. . . [Cassidy] located three men he wanted [to join his Wild
Bunch]. Kid Curry quick and fearless of no man or devil was
his first man with a deadly shot. To Curry human life meant
nothing. quite different from Cassidy. He did not look for
trouble but did not wast time if it came his way. Cassidy
would go a long way to avoid trouble not from fear but pol-
icy. Robing a bank meant nothing but Killing in cold blood
was another, and which he did not aprove. Cassidy would
rather out wit the persuers but Curry would kill if they followed to close."

kill and at that point Cassidy and Maxwell [Sundance]
[shot] Two Soldiers. Where Cassidy and Maxwell were hiding they could get good aim and was much protected from
the firing of the soldiers.

After fifteen or more soldiers were killed and several
wounded. the fireing seased for a while as the soldiers
knew it was instant death to come out in open fire. Such
deadly fire had never been seen before. Later on in the
evening, Hains was wounded and with what care Maxwell
& Cassidy could give him helped for a while, but, finaly, he

was Weakened from loss of Blood and slumped in an expand position and was shot by the soldiers.

That left Maxwell and Cassidy to fight their way out. Later on Maxwell recived a shot through the body and a scalp wound. Butch managed to get to Maxwells side and began to give him what aid he could. but Maxwell had been hard hit and Butch saw at once the best he could do was to make him as comfortable as possible as they lay there behind the rocks. Maxwell gave Butch a letter from Betty and requested him to notify [her] of his death in case he got away. He also informed Butch that Betty was his legal wife and had been for many years.

. . . It finaly grew dark and Maxwell [gave] a long sigh and said, "Good by butch my old pal dont forget Betty. take my belt with you if you can get away and send it to little Betty and she will know I died fighting and thinking of her." And with these last words he quietly passed on.

Butch had seen many people die but never did any thing affect him as did the passing of his old Friend, Maxwell.

. . . In the darkness [Butch] removed Maxwells money belt and buckled it about his own body and then [began] to think of a plan by which he hoped might gain the summet of the Canyon wall. And once on top he might evade the troop. which he knew were some where up there among the rocks. . . .

For an hour he cralled on his hands & knees so he could not be seen or heard so easily and every now & then he would stop and listen careffuly for any possible sound. . . .

Locating his own horse he removed all the food from the saddle packs and filling his own, and roaling the remainder in his coat he tied it with the bags and water bottles on the back of his saddle. Then, he & horse made their way slowly to the head of the Gorge.

According to William Phillips, Butch Cassidy made it out of South America. He then went to Liverpool, England, and later to Paris. There he had surgery to change his appearance so no one would recognize him.

Butch's last act in "The Bandit Invincible" was to write an old girlfriend in the United States. He wanted to meet her someplace. Phillips says: "[Butch] got a room in a comfortable hotel wrote a letter to his sweet heart in Calif. telling of his intintions and where to meet him in the united states Retired for the night defying any one to identify him."

If "The Bandit Invincible" is a true story, who was the woman Butch called his "sweet heart"? Is there any evidence she actually existed? And what about Butch's facial surgery? Could he have changed his appearance? If so, why did the residents of Lander, Wyoming, claim to have recognized him? Investigating these issues might have helped Larry Pointer solve the Butch Cassidy mystery.

5 Is the Mystery Solved?

Using the final details of "The Bandit Invincible," Larry Pointer has possibly found hard evidence that William Phillips was indeed Butch Cassidy. Pointer studied photographs of the two men to see whether they looked like one another. Witnesses had already told him that both men had striking blue eyes. The photographs showed more similarities. In his book Pointer states: "the resemblance was immediately apparent. It was no wonder Wyoming pioneers thought Phillips was the notorious leader of the Hole-in-the-Wall Gang."

But what about Phillips's claims that the real Butch Cassidy had altered his appearance? Larry Pointer submitted his photographs

Similar Shooting Skills

Christian Heiden of Salt Lake City was fourteen when he met Butch Cassidy, who was working at a nearby ranch. In Charles Kelly's book, The Outlaw Trail, *he describes Butch's demeanor with a gun:*

"I never saw Butch shoot anyone, but he always packed a wicked-looking Colt .45 with a big wooden handle on it. He was very quick in his actions and quick-witted."

Compare this to Ben Fitzharris's remarks on William Phillips's shooting skills in Larry Pointer's book, In Search of Butch Cassidy:

"We'd get about 20 feet from a tree and he'd put a little piece of paper up and squeeze the trigger. Boy, he could really bear down—pull down and bam! He really was a marksman. I'd try it and I'd land back on my bottom."

to an expert for analysis. This expert believes that William Phillips might have undergone facial surgery. Pointer says:

> For a professional comparison of the Phillips and Cassidy photographs, internationally renowned realist sculptor Harry Jackson was prevailed upon. Jackson believed the pictures were of the same man, pointing to basic bone structure patterns. The sculptor also expressed the opinion that the man very well could have undergone a face lift, noting the ears, especially, appeared altered.

Butch's Girlfriend

Pointer then turned his attention to the mysterious woman mentioned at the end of "The Bandit Invincible," Butch's "sweet heart in Calif." This same girlfriend is mentioned in other parts of the manuscript as living near Lander, Wyoming. Pointer suspected that the final reference to California might have been a belated attempt to conceal the woman's true identity. After all, Phillips himself admitted to having altered locations in his book.

Following this clue, Pointer discovered that while Butch had several girlfriends during his outlaw days, only one lived in Lander. Her name was Mary Boyd, the sister of Will Boyd. Two of Will Boyd's nephews, Roy Jones and Herman LaJeunesse, confirm that Mary and Butch had been romantically involved. Pointer writes:

> The two men said Butch Cassidy and Will Boyd had been close friends when Cassidy first came into the Lander area as a cowboy, and that Will's sister, Mary Boyd, had been Cassidy's sweetheart during those early years. Will also had told his nephews that Cassidy often found refuge in the Boyd home during his later years as an outlaw.

In 1895, while Butch was in the Wyoming State Penitentiary, Mary Boyd married someone else. But Mary's relatives say that she never truly ended her relationship with the outlaw. After Butch was released from prison, she often met with him in secret.

Mary was still married in 1908, the time when "The Bandit Invincible" says Butch left South America. The earliest information about William Phillips is from that same year. He appeared in Adrian, Michigan, that spring. Shortly after arriving in Adrian, he met and fell in love with Gertrude Livesay, who quickly became

William Phillips, circa 1930

Mrs. William T. Phillips. Could this be why Butch never returned to Mary Boyd?

Pointer believes so. He learned from Boyd's relatives that William Phillips met with Mary during his 1934 visit to Wyoming. Mary's brother Will arranged the meeting; Roy Jones witnessed it. Jones told Pointer he had no doubt that this meeting was the reunion of the two sweethearts. The couple shared many old memories, and eventually it became clear that Phillips was really Butch Cassidy. Boyd's family decided to keep this information to themselves.

Handwriting Analysis

In continuing his research, Pointer discovered some old letters that William Phillips had written to Mary Boyd. He then obtained a copy of a letter written by Butch Cassidy. He sent his documents to a legally certified handwriting expert, Jeannine Zimmerman.

Zimmerman examined the letters carefully and determined that William Phillips and Butch Cassidy had the same handwriting. She wrote Pointer about her findings. Her report states:

> At your request, I have examined and compared the following material:
>
> (1) Copy of a letter [from Butch Cassidy] addressed to Mrs. Davis, Ashley, Utah, dated August 10, 1902; and
> (2) Copy of a letter signed, W. T. Phillips, and dated December 17, 1935
>
> Several hours were spent in examining the style, relative size and proportions of strokes, line quality, skill ability; the appearance of pick-up strokes, connectors, terminal strokes and all other writing habits characteristic of the writer, as demonstrated in the document (1) outlined above. A comparison was then made with the handwriting of the second letter, document (2) above. Although there is

a time lapse of 33 years between the execution of the hand-writing on these two documents, many identifying characteristics noted in document (1) above were also evident in the later writing, (2) above. It is therefore my opinion that both of these documents, (1) and (2) outlined above, were executed by the same individual. I have made many notes on stroke comparisons in the examination of these two documents and would be glad to demonstrate these comparisons to you personally, as well as any other interested party.

Hard Evidence

In addition to the handwriting analysis, Larry Pointer believes he has other evidence that proves William T. Phillips was Butch Cassidy. Pointer has studied items that Phillips once owned and discovered clues to the man's identity.

Shortly before his death, Phillips sent Mary an unusual ring. Its stone was a Mexican fire opal. Phillips mailed her the ring secretly so that no one would find out about his relationship with Mary. He

The Mexican fire opal ring that Mary Boyd received from William Phillips. Larry Pointer believes that the inscription proves that Phillips and Cassidy were the same man.

wrote her about the ring in December 1935, saying, "One of my old friends from Montana came to see me the other day and is going to take me down town today to mail this as I never trust any one to mail my letters. I dont want them to know any thing of my affairs you understand."

Mary referred to this ring in a letter she sent after Phillips's death. The two had been corresponding for a long time, and when he suddenly stopped writing, she suspected the worst. She wrote to William L. Fields in Spokane, who knew of her relationship with Phillips. In part, her letter said:

> I am writing you a few lines asking you to give me a little information would you answer the questions i want to [k]now you [k]now i received letters from Mr. W. T. Phillips all the time I . . . received a letter from Mr. Phillips about a month ago send me his ring he wore 55 years ago for a keepsake is he dead i heard he was if he is i want to [k]now.

When Mary herself died, she gave the ring to her daughter. It was eventually passed on to her granddaughter, Ione Manning of Casper, Wyoming. Manning found the ring and showed it to Larry

William Phillips's revolver with Butch Cassidy's brand carved onto the pistol grip. Does the fact that Phillips owned the revolver prove he was Butch Cassidy?

William Phillips Visits Wyoming

Ben Fitzharris drove William Phillips to Lander, Wyoming, in 1934. In Larry Pointer's book, In Search of Butch Cassidy, Fitzharris offers this description of Phillips's visit:

"I walked down the street with him and that's where he first met this banker, the son of the original banker that knew Bill. . . . When we went across the street to the grocery store, . . . this guy threw up his hands and threw his arms around Bill and asked, 'George, how are you? . . . it's been ages.' Well, they were all taken with him. They threw their arms around him and called him 'George' and 'Cassidy, Cassidy.'

And the old marshal of Lander at that time remembered him. That's why we went across to one of those old hotels there—if you go to Lander, you'll know it, it's right across from the bank, those high ceilings you know, about thirty feet high. And we had quite a night there, with those old-timers sitting around and tossing them back. But they all knew George Cassidy."

Pointer. Inside was the inscription: "Geo C to Mary B." This discovery might have great significance. Pointer writes: "George Cassidy to Mary Boyd! Here was the first documented proof that William T. Phillips claimed to be George 'Butch' Cassidy."

Another piece of evidence might link William T. Phillips to Butch Cassidy. Phillips owned three guns. One was a .22 caliber derringer and two were Colt revolvers. On the handle of one of the revolvers was a distinguishing mark. It was an exact duplicate of a cattle brand once used by Butch Cassidy himself.

Butch's Sister Says No

Given all of this evidence, Larry Pointer has no doubt that William T. Phillips was Butch Cassidy. However, Butch's sister says he was not. In her book, *Butch Cassidy, My Brother*, she states: "Robert LeRoy Parker . . . was not the man who was known as William Phillips, reported to be Butch Cassidy."

Lula Parker Betenson adds that her brother never had a wife or a child. She says: "Although we have received a couple of reports to the contrary, so far as we know Butch was never married. I am sure that if he had been, he would have told us; and if he'd had any children, you can be sure he would have taken care of them, and we would have known."

But some of Betenson's relatives disagree. Her brother, Dan Parker, met with William Phillips in 1930. Parker's daughter-in-law, Ellnor Parker, says their meeting marked the beginning of many years of correspondence. Dan destroyed all of Phillips's letters right after reading them, but Ellnor claims he told her that Butch Cassidy lived in Spokane as William Phillips.

If this were true, why would Lula Betenson deny that William Phillips was Butch Cassidy? Perhaps she was afraid that Phillips's grave would be disturbed. In her book she talks at length about her fear of Butch's body being discovered. She says:

> Where he is buried and under what name is still our secret. Dad said, "All his life he was chased. Now he has a chance to rest in peace, and that's the way it must be." Revealing his burial place would furnish clues for the curious to crack that secret. I wouldn't be a Parker if I broke my word.

> To further emphasize my concern for keeping his burial place a secret, may I relate a significant incident. My son Mark, who runs the old Parker Ranch near Circleville, had a man doing some leveling on a part of the property. Some time previously Mark had buried his old dog Hummerdo, to which his family was greatly attached. All our lives, we've buried animals because of sentiment. So, on that particular day, Mark said to the workman, "Just stay away from the corner over there on the hill. There's a grave there, and I don't want it disturbed." Next day, Circleville was buzzing with the rumor that Butch Cassidy was buried at the ranch.

> Another well-meaning person who claims to know where the Banditti Americanos were supposed to have been buried after the battle of San Vicente wanted to contact Bolivian authorities and have their bodies exhumed and sent to me at Circleville for burial on the Parker Ranch. I have since heard that the two have been exhumed, and that saddens me. Of course, the exhumation was for identification purposes, and it proved that the two who were buried were not bandits, as had been believed. . . .

In the newspaper I have recently read that [another out-law's] body was dug up, and I was hurt to see the gruesome pictures. This exhumation has also happened to other outlaws recently.

Who knows what might spring into the minds of either some hero-worshippers or some debunkers in another fifty years? It is entirely possible that some person or persons would want to make a memorial out of my brother's burial spot if it were known. This would amount to glorifying his misspent life, an honor certainly not according to his wishes nor the wishes of the family.

If I were to reveal his burial place, someone would be sure to disturb it under some pretext, and my brother is entitled to rest in peace.

Other Experts Remain Unsure

Even though Lula Parker Betenson has a motive for denying that William Phillips was Butch Cassidy, several historians believe she is telling the truth. In his book, *Western Outlaws: The "Good Bad-*

William T. Phillips works in his machine shop, his hand sporting the fire opal ring he later gave to Mary Boyd. The Phillips adding machine is on a bench on the right.

man" in Fact, Film, and Folklore, Kent Ladd Steckmesser says Betenson's book might be accurate. However, he remains unimpressed by Larry Pointer's research. Steckmesser explains:

> Stories that Cassidy had not been killed in South America were in oral circulation for years, despite the published reports of his demise. Such stories formed the core of both the Pointer and Betenson books. Pointer investigated the possibility that William T. Phillips . . . had been Cassidy. . . . [Phillips's book, "The Bandit Invincible,"] contained so many "inside" details of the outlaw's career that a number of people believed Phillips to have been Cassidy. Pointer himself became one of those believers after analyzing all the pro and con evidence.

> Lula Parker Betenson decided to break a forty-year silence and tell the truth about her brother [that he was not William Phillips]. . . .

> Ordinarily, one would discount such stories, since they are so much a part of the classic folklore pattern. [Outlaws] Jesse James, Billy the Kid, and John Derringer had not really died; the corpses were those of look-alikes. But, after all, Mrs. Betenson was the outlaw's sister. Pointer's Mr. Phillips is a much more dubious candidate. Aside from various factual inaccuracies, about half of the Phillips manuscript describes Cassidy's acts of charity, including two Poor Widow episodes [in which Cassidy gives money to women in need]. The abundance of these anecdotes suggests that the document has folkloric rather than historical importance. In any case, speculation about the outlaw's possible return-from-the-dead helped to keep his legend alive.

Other historians think Pointer did an excellent job in solving the mystery of Butch Cassidy's death. Richard Patterson, in his book, *Train Robbery*, praises Pointer's work:

> Was this William Phillips really Butch Cassidy? The evidence is strong that he was. A Montana writer, Larry Pointer, devoted countless hours to settle the question. The results of his effort, a book entitled *In Search of Butch*

Cassidy, is a superb account of the outlaw's life. . . . After exhaustive study, Pointer concluded [that Phillips's manuscript, "The Bandit Invincible,"] was genuine, and that William Phillips and Cassidy were one and the same. Although childishly written, occasionally vague, and obviously self-serving, "The Bandit Invincible," Pointer feels, contained information only Butch would have known.

Patterson notes that Lula Parker Betenson "could have settled the matter, but she chose not to. She did admit, however, that Butch did not die in Bolivia."

So What Really Happened?

If we accept Betenson's account as the truth, then at least we know that Butch Cassidy left South America unharmed. But her story about how the outlaw escaped death is very different from the version described in William Phillips's "The Bandit Invincible." Larry Pointer's research gives this manuscript credibility. Yet "The Bandit Invincible" supports much of Arthur Chapman's article about the Bolivian shoot-out—and Chapman's article is highly suspect.

So what are we to believe? Did Larry Pointer solve the mystery of Butch Cassidy's death? Did the outlaw manage to outsmart the Pinkertons and start a new life in the United States as an honest man? Was he William T. Phillips?

At the time of Phillips's death, many who knew him thought the idea was ridiculous. In an article published in the Spokane *Spokesman-Review* on July 23, 1940, attorney Lucius G. Nash said: "I knew William Phillips well and he had often visited in my home. As a lawyer, I have my own method of looking at this thing. Nobody can make me believe Phillips was Butch Cassidy."

Yet in Lander, Wyoming, they tell an interesting story about William T. Phillips. While he was visiting there in 1934, he went on a pack trip through the Wind River Mountains. People who went with him say he was always heading off by himself. He kept digging holes under the north sides of trees and often complained about how much the countryside had changed.

Legend has it that in 1896 Butch Cassidy and Elzy Lay buried money from the Montpelier bank robbery someplace near the Wind River Mountains. What was William T. Phillips looking for?

For Further Reading

Charles Dixon Anderson, *Outlaws of the Old West*. Los Angeles: Mankind Publishing Company, 1973. This book for advanced readers offers biographical information about many Old West figures, including Butch Cassidy, Belle Starr, Billy the Kid, Black Bart, and Wild Bill Hickok.

James L. Collins, *Lawmen of the Old West*. New York: Franklin Watts, 1990. This book for young readers tells about the lawmen who lived in the frontier towns of the Old West.

Gail Drago, *Etta Place: Her Life and Times with the Sundance Kid*. Plano: Republic of Texas Press, 1995. This biography of Etta Place is part of a series for advanced readers entitled "Women of the West."

Janet Serlin Garber, *The Mystery of Butch Cassidy and the Sundance Kid*. New York: Contemporary Perspectives, 1979. This book for young readers offers a biography of the two outlaws and discusses the mystery of their death.

Carl R. Green, *Butch Cassidy*. Springfield, NJ: Enslow Publishers, 1995. This biography is part of a series for young people entitled "Outlaws and Lawmen of the Wild West."

John Hamilton, *Butch Cassidy*. Minneapolis: Abdo & Daughters, 1996. This biography is part of a series for young people entitled "Heroes and Villains of the Wild West."

D. J. Herda, *Outlaws of the American West*. Brookfield, CT: Millbrook Press, 1995. This book for young readers discusses the most famous outlaws of the American West between 1848 and 1890.

James D. Horan, *The Pinkertons: The Detective Dynasty That Made History*. New York: Crown, 1967. For the more advanced reader, this book offers a thorough history of the famous detective agency and the cases it solved.

James D. Horan and Paul Sann, *Pictorial History of the Wild West: A True Account of the Bad Men, Desperadoes, Rustlers, and Outlaws of the Old West—and the Men Who Fought Them to Establish Law and Order*. New York: Crown, 1954. This book offers many excellent pictures of famous Old West figures.

Edward M. Kirby, *The Rise and Fall of the Sundance Kid.* Iola, WI: Western Publications, 1983. For the more advanced reader, this book offers biographical information about the Sundance Kid.

Grant Lyons, *Mustangs, Six-Shooters and Barbed Wire.* New York: Julian Messner, 1981. This book for young readers offers a brief history of the settling of the American West, offering a glimpse into pioneer life.

Allan Pinkerton, *Thirty Years a Detective.* Montclair, NJ: Patterson Smith, 1975. For the more advanced reader, this book offers a glimpse into Allan Pinkerton's life as the founder of the famous Pinkerton National Detective Agency. It was originally written in 1884 by Pinkerton himself.

Gail Stewart, *Where Lies Butch Cassidy?* New York: Crestwood House, 1992. This book for young readers summarizes the controversy over Butch Cassidy's death.

Frank Surge, *Western Lawmen*, Minneapolis: Lerner, 1969. This book for young readers gives short biographical information about some famous lawmen and outlaws of the Old West.

Diane Yancey, *Desperadoes and Dynamite: Train Robbery in the United States.* New York: Franklin Watts, 1991. This book for young readers includes many interesting stories about several notorious train robbers, including Jesse James, the Dalton Gang, and Butch Cassidy and the Sundance Kid.

Video

William Goldman, *Butch Cassidy and the Sundance Kid.* This 1969 movie by Twentieth Century Fox starring Paul Newman and Robert Redford is now available on home video.

Works Consulted

Pearl Baker, *The Wild Bunch at Robbers Roost.* New York: Abelard-Schuman, 1971. This book tells about life at Robbers Roost from the perspective of a woman who actually lived there and knew Butch Cassidy and his Wild Bunch.

Lula Parker Betenson, as told to Dora Flack, *Butch Cassidy, My Brother.* Provo, UT: Brigham Young University Press, 1975. This is the story of Butch's life as seen through the eyes of his younger sister.

E. Richard Churchill, *The McCartys: They Rode with Butch Cassidy.* Leadville, CO: Timberline Books, 1972. This booklet recounts the exploits of the notorious McCarty brothers, who were once members of Butch's Wild Bunch.

James D. Horan, *Desperate Men.* New York: Doubleday, 1949. This well-researched book offers biographical information about several Old West outlaws.

Charles Kelly, *The Outlaw Trail: A History of Butch Cassidy and His Wild Bunch.* New York: Devin-Adair Company, 1959. This book is a revised edition of the first biography of Butch Cassidy, written by Kelly in 1938.

Richard Patterson, *Train Robbery.* Denver: Johnson Publishing Company, 1981. This book discusses the history of train robbery in the United States, and offers biographical information about outlaws like Butch Cassidy.

Larry Pointer, *In Search of Butch Cassidy.* Norman: University of Oklahoma Press, 1977. This book focuses on the controversy over Butch Cassidy's death and offers excerpts from the manuscript of William T. Phillips, whom Pointer believed was really Butch Cassidy in his later years.

Robert Redford, *The Outlaw Trail: A Journey Through Time.* New York: Grosset and Dunlap, 1978. This book, written by one of the stars of the movie *Butch Cassidy and the Sundance Kid,* offers many photographs of the area where Butch and his Wild Bunch rode, along with a travelogue and historical facts about the region.

Kent Ladd Steckmesser, *Western Outlaws: The "Good Badman" in Fact, Film, and Folklore.* Claremont, CA: Regina Books, 1983. This book discusses the way the American people view their notorious Old West outlaws.

Brown Waller, *Last of the Great Western Train Robbers.* South Brunswick, NY: A. S. Barnes, 1968. This book offers biographical information about several famous train robbers.

Matt Warner, as told to Murray E. King. *Last of the Bandit Riders.* New York: Bonanza, 1938. This book tells the story of the Wild Bunch through the eyes of Matt Warner, one of the bandits who rode with Butch Cassidy.

Index

Aramayo mines (Bolivia), 27
Argentina, 37–39
  Cassidy's robbery sites in, 40

Baker, Pearl, 45
Baldwin, Jim, 70
bandidos Yanquis, 38, 42, 44
"The Bandit Invincible"
  (Phillips), 65, 66, 67
  truth of, 69–70
Bank of Loudres and Tarapaca
  robbery (Argentina), 38
Beattie, J. A., 15
Betenson, Lula Parker, 7, 22,
  36, 38, 40, 54
  account of Cassidy's death,
    33–34
  on Cassidy's return from
    South America, 52
  denies identity of Phillips as
    Cassidy, 81–82
  motives for, 82
  on Seibert's story, 47–48
Billings Gazette, 56
Bolivia, 26, 27
  Cassidy's escape to, 38
  police records in, 43
  story of Cassidy's death in,
    27–30
Bowman, Henry, 55
Boyd, Mary, 77
  ring from William Phillips,
    79–81
Brown's Park, 15
Butch Cassidy, My Brother
  (Betenson), 7, 22, 34, 38, 52,
  81

*Butch Cassidy and the
  Sundance Kid*, 35

Calverly, Bob, 18
Calvert, Mary, 50
Carver, Bill, 20
Cassidy, George "Butch"
  admiration of, 6
  in Argentina, 37, 39, 40
  escape to Bolivia, 38
  attitude toward Mormon
    Church, 9
  begins life of crime, 9–10
  birth of, 6
  changes name, 11–12
  death of
    Chapman's story, 27–30
    "Mr. Steele's" story, 42–43
    rumors about, 38–41
  facial surgery of, 74, 76–77
  first bank robbery, 12–15
  flight to South America,
    26–27
  friendship with Percy Seibert,
    45–47
  identity as William Phillips,
    57
    handwriting comparison,
      78–79
    Mary Boyd's ring as
      evidence of, 79–81
  in Mexico, rumors about,
    54–56
  reported sightings of, 53
  visit to Lander, Wyoming, 50
  at Wyoming State
    Penitentiary, 19

prison record at, 21
Cassidy, Mike, 10
Cassidy Point, 15
cattle rustling, 10–11
Chapman, Arthur, 45, 72
  source of information, 36, 47
  story of Cassidy's death,
    27–30
  acceptance as fact, 30–32,
    52
  criticism of, 32–34
Christensen, Mart T., 49, 57
  letter to Charles Kelly, 51
Churchill, E. Richard, 11, 15
Circle Valley (Utah), 7
Clarin, 44
Clark, Jim, 16
Concordia Tin Mines (Bolivia),
  26, 45
Curry, Kid, 20, 73

Desperate Men (Horan), 9
Dilley, Tom, 42
Dimaio, Frank P., 37, 42

Early Days in Wyoming
  (Walker), 56
Ekker, Arthur, 49
Elks Magazine, 27
Evans, Robert, 44

Fields, William L., 80
Fitzharris, Ben, 81

Glasgow, Blanche Lundstrom,
  65, 67
Goldman, William, 35
Great Red Wall, 20
Grimmett, Orson, 70

Harriman, E.H., 23
Harris, Ellen, 66
Heiden, Christian, 76
Hole-in-the-Wall, 19
Horan, James, 9

In Search of Butch Cassidy
  (Pointer), 16, 31, 39, 44, 46,
  51, 57, 59, 81

James, Jesse, 52
Johnson, William G., 50, 57, 60

Kelly, Charles, 6, 10, 17, 18, 34,
  42, 63
  attitude toward Christensen's
    research, 50–52
  on Cassidy's living in Idaho,
    56
  dismissal of "Cassidy in
    Mexico" story, 54–56
  research on William Phillips,
    58–59
  on rumors of Cassidy's death,
    53–54
Kelly, John F., 9
Kilpatrick, Ben, 20

Lander, Wyoming, 50, 51, 56,
  70, 77, 85
Last of the Bandit Riders
  (Warner), 24
Lay, Elzy, 20, 22, 25, 34, 35, 42,
  50, 85
Lincoln, Abraham, 23
Livesay, Gertrude. *See* Phillips,
  Gertrude
Logan, Harry, 20, 44
Longabaugh, Harry, 20, 27, 37,
  69, 73

death of, 74
Chapman's story, 27
flight to South America, 26

Manning, Ione, 80
Marshall, Jim, 10
The McCartys: They Rode with Butch Cassidy (Churchill), 11, 15
McParlan, James, 24
Meeks, Bub, 22
Mexico
rumors about Cassidy living in, 54–56
Molly Maguires, 24
Montpelier Bank robbery (Idaho), 22, 85
Mormon Church, 7, 8

Nash, Lucius G., 85
Newman, Paul, 35

Ogden, Harry, 55
The Outlaw Trail: A History of Butch Cassidy and His Wild Bunch (Kelly), 6, 10, 17, 18, 34, 42, 56, 63
The Outlaw Trail: A Journey Through Time (Redford), 15, 16, 20, 49, 57
Overland Flyer, 22

Parker, Ann, 7
Parker, Dan, 82
Parker, Maximillian, 7
Parker, Robert LeRoy. *See* Cassidy, George "Butch"
Parker Ranch, 7–8
Patterson, Richard, 84–85
Penia, Don Pedro, 44

Phillips, Gertrude, 60, 77–78
letter on husband's life, 61–63
Phillips, William T.
"The Bandit Invincible" manuscript and, 65
reasons for writing, 68–69
birth certificate of, 58–60
Butch Cassidy and handwriting comparison, 78–79
identity as, 57–60
correspondence with Dan Parker, 82
visit to Lander, Wyoming, 50, 81
Piernes, Justo, 44
Pinkerton, Allan, 23
Pinkerton National Detective Agency, 23, 37, 42, 48
Place, Etta, 26, 37, 45, 69
background of, 41
Pointer, Larry, 16, 31–32, 39, 44, 46, 51, 81
reactions to work of, 83–85
on truth of "The Bandit Invincible," 70
on William Phillips's birth certificate, 59–60

Redford, Robert, 15, 16, 20, 35, 49, 57
Robbers Roost, 16, 17, 40
Robinson, Edna, 20
Rock Springs, Wyoming, 17, 18

San Miguel Bank Robbery (Telluride, Colorado), 12–15
San Vicente, Bolivia, 27
rumors of graves near, 44

Seibert, Percy, 45–47
Siringo, Charles, 24
Spokane Spokesman-Review,
    85
Steckmesser, Kent Ladd, 34, 84
the Sundance Kid. *See*
    Longabaugh, Harry

Telluride, Colorado, 11, 16
Thirty Years a Detective
    (Pinkerton), 23
Train Robbery (Patterson),
    84–85

Union Pacific Railroad, 22, 23

Walker, Tacetta B., 50
    letter to Kelly, 56
Warner, Matt, 24, 54
Washington Post, 27
*Western Outlaws: The "Good
    Badman" in Fact, Film, and*

Folklore (Steckmesser), 34,
    83–84
Wild Bunch
    first train robbery, 22
    formation of, 19–20
    last crime by, 25
    members of, 20
    robberies committed by, 14
    *The Wild Bunch at Robbers
        Roost* (Baker), 45
Wilson, Williams, 44
Woodcock, Earnest C., 22
Wyoming State Penitentiary,
    19, 77
    Cassidy's prison record at, 21
Wyoming State Tribune, 18
Wyoming Writers Project, 49

Zimmerman, Jeannine, 78

Picture Credits

Cover photos: Denver Public Library, Western History Department

American Heritage Center, University of Wyoming, 58, 59, 62, 64, 78, 79, 80, 83

Bettmann, 7

Colorado Historical Society, 13

Denver Public Library, Western History Department, 10, 17, 20, 22, 26, 28

Library of Congress, 23

Peter Newark's Western Americana, 25, 38, 46, 67

Springer/Bettmann Film Archive, 35

UPI/Bettmann, 32

Utah State Historical Society, 71

Wyoming Division of Cultural Resources, 19, 21, 43, 51

About the Author

Patricia Netzley received a bachelor's degree in English from the University of California at Los Angeles (UCLA). After graduation she worked as an editor at the UCLA Medical Center, where she produced hundreds of medical articles, speeches, and pamphlets.

Netzley became a freelance writer in 1986. She is the author of three other nonfiction books for young people, *The Assassination of President John F. Kennedy* (Macmillan/New Discovery Books, 1994), *The Importance of Queen Victoria* (Lucent Books, 1996), and *Alien Abductions* (Lucent Books, 1997).

Netzley and her husband Raymond live in Southern California with their three children, Matthew, Sarah, and Jacob.